# Manfred von Richthofen

# Manfred von Richthofen

## His Life and Times in Pictures

Tim Hillier-Graves

AIR WORLD

First published in Great Britain in 2024 by
Pen & Sword Air World
An imprint of Pen & Sword Books Limited
Yorkshire – Philadelphia

ISBN 978 1 03610 031 5

A CIP catalogue record for this book is
available from the British Library

Typeset by Mac Style
Printed in the UK by CPI Group (UK) Ltd, Croydon, CR0 4YY.

Pen & Sword Books Limited incorporates the imprints of After the Battle,
Atlas, Archaeology, Aviation, Discovery, Family History, Fiction, History,
Maritime, Military, Military Classics, Politics, Select, Transport, True Crime,
Air World, Frontline Publishing, Leo Cooper, Remember When, Seaforth
Publishing, The Praetorian Press, Wharncliffe Local History, Wharncliffe
Transport, Wharncliffe True Crime and White Owl.

For a complete list of Pen & Sword titles please contact:

PEN & SWORD BOOKS LIMITED
47 Church Street, Barnsley, South Yorkshire, S70 2AS, England
E-mail: enquiries@pen-and-sword.co.uk
Website: www.pen-and-sword.co.uk
or
PEN AND SWORD BOOKS
1950 Lawrence Rd, Havertown, PA 19083, USA
E-mail: uspen-and-sword@casematepublishers.com
Website: www.penandswordbooks.com

# Contents

# Acknowledgements

The old saying that 'a picture is worth a thousand words' is undoubtedly true, but it is a process helped considerably by knowing the subject and the circumstances under which each photograph was taken. This is particularly so when a picture portrays scenes of war. It is easy to look back with sympathy and quickly pass on, much harder to truly understand the enormity of what is happening. To do this we often need someone who can guide us through the speculation and misconceptions that can cloud our understanding of events.

It also helps if this guide can give the reader a broad understanding of time and place, assisted, wherever possible, by the words of those who were there and witnessed these events first-hand. In this book I have assumed this role and hope that I haven't fallen short or made mistakes in attribution or assumed something that may be incorrect or is open to debate.

As a supplement to my *Manfred von Richthofen – The High Price of Glory*, this book shares many of the same contributors. Some of these simply helped me understand what it felt like to fight for one's country, while others provided me with photographs, memories or other reference material to help illuminate the story of his short life. Rather than repeat all the names here I have listed those whose contribution to this book have been most significant:

Ronald Adams, Thomas Cassidy, Joseph Fall, Bill Foster, Albert Graves, Bernard Graves, John Hawkins, Tim Hervey, Albert Heurteaux, Arthur Hillier, Arthur Gould Lee, Cecil Lewis, David Lewis, Neville MacNamara, Jack Moses, Hans-Georg von de Osten, Dennis Renvoize, Leonard 'Tich' Rochford, Karl-August von Schoenebeck and Mike Tritton.

I was also given much assistance in my research by four historians who made it their lifetime's work to collect information about Great War aviators and von Richthofen in particular. In the USA there were Charles Donald, Pasquale Carisella and Ed Ferko, all now long dead. They were all very generous in their help and sent me masses of material over the years and answered my many questions with great patience. Then there was Douglas Whetton, who died tragically at an early age, but had, in a very short time, gathered a great deal of unique material that he, then his family, shared with me.

To all those who helped research and then prepare this book I offer my thanks.

A commemorative plaque that appeared after the 1918 war and proved hugely popular in a country that had, like all warring nations, grown tired of this terrible conflict. Von Richthofen, even in these difficult times, could still conjure up a vision of chivalry and knightly virtue to be admired. (*Author*)

# Introduction

Richthofen flew and fought for his Kaiser and his fatherland from a strong sense of duty and responsibility, not for personal reward, no matter what the cost … He was a born leader … He saw everything in the air and on the ground. He protected every member of his Geschwader as a matter of course, but did not forgive someone if he turned away from a fight … He was the bravest man I ever knew. His death in April 1918 affected all who knew him very deeply as it did Germany as a whole. We could ill-afford to lose a man of such courage, awareness and common sense and badly needed him in the decades that followed.

So wrote Hans-Georg von der Osten in a letter to the author when recalling a man whose life had so profoundly affected his own. As an inexperienced fighter pilot, von der Osten joined JG I led by Manfred von Richthofen in August 1917 and grew to maturity under his calm, inspiring leadership.

Von der Osten was not alone in his admiration of the *Der Rote Kamplieger*, as he was known in Germany, or *Le Petite Rouge*, in grudging admiration by his enemies. In fact, there seems to have been no one else in this terrible war whose name and reputation became so revered that it crossed patriotic, often xenophobic, boundaries. In a conflict that saw propaganda used on susceptible minds, to evoke hatred of the enemy, this is quite remarkable. And it might help explain the reaction of the British press in reporting his 'victories' as though they were part of a sporting event, not the deaths of their fellow countrymen. Then, when he was killed on 21 April 1918, they avoided a tone of triumphalism in their obituaries by using such words as 'a gallant foe' and 'a brave and chivalrous enemy', to describe his life and deeds.

The warrior at the height of his fame and a national hero without equal in Germany – Manfred von Richthofen in the early summer of 1917, before exhaustion and a severe head wound took their toll of his health and well-being. (*Author*)

Even more surprising was the lack of censure when the Royal Air Force, which came into being that month, gave von Richthofen a full military funeral and honour guard, all of which was reported on front pages with some piety and little moralising by British journalists. In the circumstances a most unusual and surprising outcome, but a topic

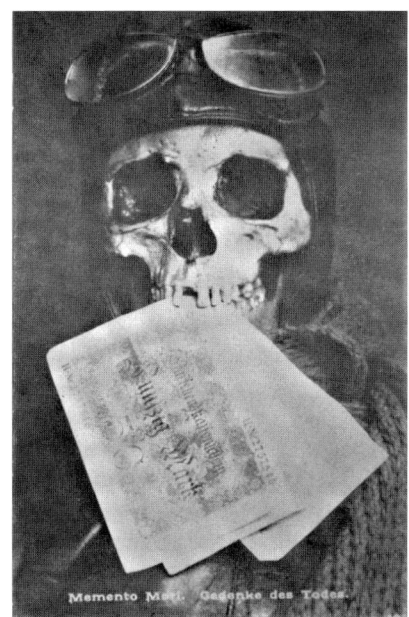

The black humour of the fighting man is captured in this popular German postcard of 1917–18, which makes play of the 5 Marks paid each day as danger money to aircrew. Life in war is a cheap, easily sacrificed commodity. (*Author*)

unlikely to have found much sympathy with the relatives of the many men he killed or wounded as a fighter pilot, or so you would think. But in 1914–18 few, if any, could choose whether to fight or not, the moral obligation being overwhelmingly applied by a rigid, uncompromising leadership and a long-established militaristic and ethical code rigorously harnessed by in all the warring nations.

'My country right and wrong' seemed an honourable philosophy at the time, but in a world of empires and few civil liberties, it was a model too easily abused in pursuit of national glory. As a result, millions died or were crippled in a war that could so easily have been avoided. As this tragedy slowly unfolded, each side sought the moral high ground as the suffering grew steadily worse, with propaganda their primary tool. In many ways Germany lagged behind Britain and France in this endeavour, where stories quickly spread describing the opposition's barbaric behaviour so giving birth to the image of 'the Ghastly Hun'. At first the German High Command was slow to respond. Then, in late 1916, all this changed when Field Marshal Paul von Hindenburg and General Erich Ludendorff became Germany's supreme war lords.

The universally recognised symbol of the air war on the Western Front in mid-1917 – an Albatros D.III, thought to be flown by von Richthofen, comes into land. In the capable hands of experienced fighter pilots these biplanes dominated the skies for a time. (*CD = Charles Donald*)

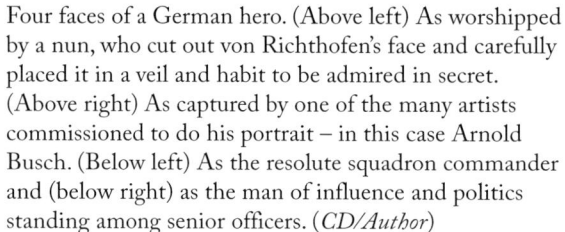

Four faces of a German hero. (Above left) As worshipped by a nun, who cut out von Richthofen's face and carefully placed it in a veil and habit to be admired in secret. (Above right) As captured by one of the many artists commissioned to do his portrait – in this case Arnold Busch. (Below left) As the resolute squadron commander and (below right) as the man of influence and politics standing among senior officers. (*CD/Author*)

With severe shortages at home and huge losses at the front crippling its war effort, Germany's propagandists, led by Walter Nicolai, Ludendorff's most astute spymaster and manipulator of news, chose to influence opinion by building up the reputations of the country's heroes. It proved to be a successful policy that soon drew on the experiences of aviators and fighter pilots for its inspiration.

To a certain extent the novelty of flying was still newsworthy and in 1915 and 1916 the names of Oswald Boelcke, Max Immelmann, Otto Parschau and Kurt Wintgens, among others, began to fill many column inches. The attention they attracted quickly elevated them to the status of national heroes, but the fragility of life in such a hostile environment was soon exposed and as these aviators began to fall so their propaganda value diminished. Nevertheless, Ludendorff and Nicolai persevered with this policy and in late 1916 a new, seemingly invincible hero emerged in the form of one young Uhlan cavalry officer – Manfred von Richthofen. And so, the legend of *Der Rote Kampfflieger* was born with a potency so strong it still resonates with us today.

# Part 1

# May 1892 to April 1915

Manfred's father, Albrecht, was born on 13 November 1859, the eldest son of Karl Oscar Lothar von Richthofen, who owned and worked an estate at Romberg near Breslau in Silesia. Albrecht's mother, Hulda Eva von Teichmann, hailed from the Mecklenburg region of northern Germany and was undoubtedly attracted to the notably handsome, well-established Karl, who would have been considered 'quite a catch' for any young woman at the time. Their eldest child, Albrecht, chose to enter the Corps of Cadets and joined the 12th Regiment of Uhlans. How his father greeted this news is not recorded, but it was an honourable career so was probable accepted without reproach.

Manfred's mother, Kunigunde von Schickfuss und Neudorff, came from an equally privileged background, her father Leopold owning Baumgarten, a substantial estate to the south of Breslau. It was while under the tutelage of Baron von Falkenhausen of Wallisfurth, when learning about estate management, that Leopold fell for and married Maria Theresia von Falkenhausen, one of the baron's four daughters. The marriage produced Kunigunde on 27 November 1868 and her sister, Elfriede, two years later.

In an age where women, even those of her class, had few rights and were simply expected to marry and bear children, finding a suitable husband was essential. The route to a good marriage for young woman such as Kunigunde was a traditional one for noble families such as hers. Eligible young women were promenaded at social events where eligible young men, with title, rank or wealth, were present. In Kunigunde's case Albrecht von Richthofen appeared to have all three and so was quickly found acceptable.

Marriage soon followed, but if it was expected that Karl von Richthofen's wealth would pass to his eldest son, a surprise was in store. With two other sons, Friedrich and Walter Lothar, to support, plus his wife, the income from his assets seems to have proved inadequate. And when Karl died in 1893 there seems to have been insufficient value in his estate for Albrecht to receive an inheritance of any sort. So, he and his wife had to manage on an army officer's pay and they struggled as their family grew larger.

Albrecht and Kunigunde's relationship soon began to show cracks, with the lack of assets at its root. Any differences they had were probably aggravated by the arrival of their daughter Elisabeth 'Ilse' Therese Elfriede in August 1890. At this stage the couple were living in Kleinburg, on the south-eastern edge of Breslau, close to where Albrecht's regiment, the Kurassier Regiment Grosser Kurfurst Nr. 1, was quartered. There has been some speculation that the building in which they lived was part of large apartment block on the Kaiser-Wilhelm Strasse. If so it was here that Manfred Albrecht was born on 2

The von Richthofen line. (Top row left to right) Manfred's grandfather Karl 'Julius' von Richthofen, who died in Breslau during 1893 aged 75. Manfred's father Albrecht and (lower row, left to right) younger brothers Friedrich-Wilhelm, who lived until 1955, and Walter, who migrated to the USA, where he died in May 1898. (*CD*)

(Top picture) Thought to be the block of apartments on Kaiser-Wilhelm Strasse in Breslau where Manfred was born in May 1892. (Lower pictures, left to right) Kunigunde von Schickfuss und Neudorff as she would have appeared when marrying Albrecht von Richthofen. Manfred as a small boy wearing the accepted clothes of the day whether a child was a boy or a girl. (*CD/Author*)

(Left to right) With his sister, Ilse, taking a back seat and a liveried servant on hand, Manfred takes the reins. On the death of her father in 1903 Kunigunde inherited sufficient funds from his estate for her and Albrecht to buy a new family home in Schweidnitz (lower left, here photographed in 2005 when in a dilapidated condition). Manfred (lower right) photographed shortly before departing for the Prussian Cadet Institute at Wahlstatt in 1903. (*CD/Author*)

May 1892, with his brother, Lothar Siegfried, arriving two years later on 27 September 1894. Finally, a fourth and last child, Bolko, was born after quite a long gap in 1903.

The family's financial problems grew even worse when, during a winter exercise, Albrecht, now a major, suffered a significant health problem, as Manfred recalled:

My father was the most conscientious soldier imaginable. He began to suffer from difficulty of hearing and had to resign. He contracted ear trouble when saving one of his men from drowning, and though he was wet through and through he insisted upon continuing his duties as if nothing had happened, wet as he was, without taking notice of the rigours of the weather.

As a result of this, Albrecht suffered a loss of hearing that meant leaving the army. As a soldier his income barely covered their needs, and living on a pension made things even worse. However, a hearing impairment didn't stop Albrecht seeking other work and he found employment in nearby Schweidnitz procuring horses for the army. In due course, this meant a move away from Breslau and a new home.

Kunigunde's father died in 1903 and sufficient funds were forthcoming from his estate to allow her and Albrecht to buy a large house in Schweidnitz overlooking a park in which to raise their family.

Up to then Kunigunde's children had undergone home schooling, supplemented later on by attendance at a local school, which may account for Manfred's lack of academic prowess. But extra-curricular activities, of which there were many in the countryside for him to enjoy, focussed on open-air pastimes, which seem to have been closer to his heart. So hunting and riding, and the pursuits of a country gentleman, increasingly absorbed him, turning him into a tough, capable, resilient young man.

When Manfred reached the age of 11 a decision was made over his future. His father seemed determined that his sons would follow military careers and Manfred was soon despatched to the Prussian Cadet Institute at Wahlstatt, in Silesia. However, being a boy of spirit, with a strong sense of independence, he found a life subordinated to a bullying, often petty military regime difficult to accept. His response was, inevitably, a poor one, as he later reported:

I did just enough work to pass. In my opinion it would have been wrong to do more than just sufficient, so I worked as little as possible. The consequence was that my teachers did not think overmuch of me. On the other hand, I was very fond of sport, particularly gymnastics, football etc. I could do all possible tricks on the horizontal bar.

I had a tremendous fondness for all sorts of risky tricks. One fine day I climbed, with my friend Frankenberg, up the well-known steeple at Wahlstatt by means of the lightning conductor and tied my handkerchief to the top.

(Opposite top) The Prussian Cadet Institute at Wahlstatt as it appeared in the early twentieth century when Manfred was a reluctant and unhappy pupil there. (Opposite bottom) On leave from Wahlstatt with his younger brothers, Bolko (left) and Lothar. (Top, this page) When meeting Field Marshal von Hindenburg in 1917 he and Manfred, discovered that they had both occupied Study Room No. 6 whilst at Wahlstatt. Here it is captured in a contemporary photograph. (Bottom) The Friedenskirche in Schweidnitz where Manfred and his family worshipped regularly. (*CD/Author*)

From 1909 to 1911 Manfred attended the Prussian Military Academy at Lichterfelde on the edge of Berlin to train as an officer. (Top) An aerial view of the college. (Left) Manfred as a newly commissioned officer, a status he only achieved at the second attempt. (Opposite) Two contemporary views of the college demonstrating its heavy emphasis on physical activity, doing one's duty and regimentation. (*Author/CD*)

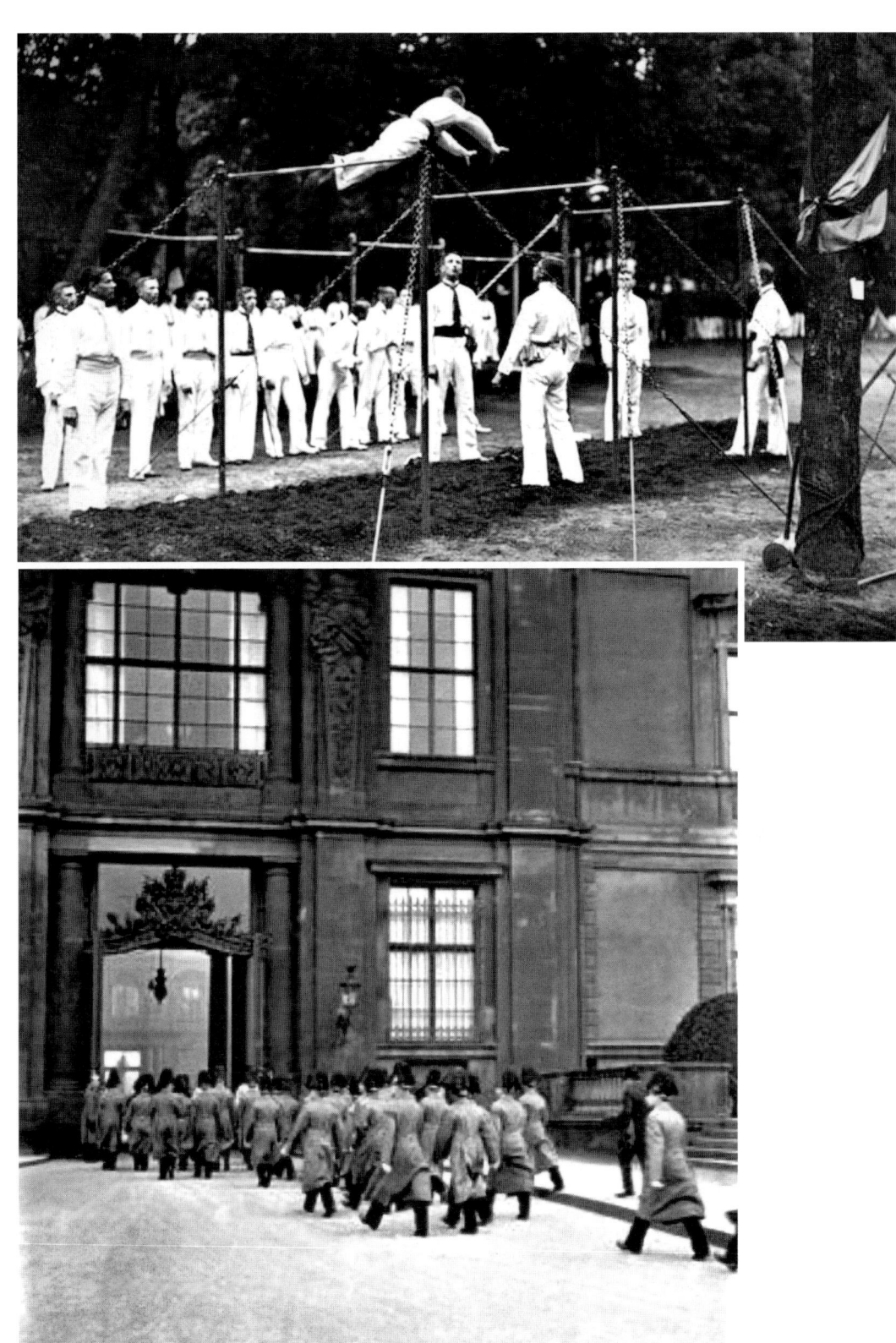

Life as an officer in a Uhlan regiment in peacetime held many attractions, riding and hunting among them. When not soldiering Manfred pursued these interests fully. (Top left) Manfred third over a water jump in a pre-war competition. (Top right) His friend and competitor Prince Friedrich Karl, a fellow officer and member of the 1912 German Olympic team. But for the war, Manfred may have joined him as an Olympian in 1916. The prince died of wounds in 1917 having become a fighter pilot. (Lower left) A cup won by Manfred in September 1911. (Lower right) The Uhlans parade before the Kaiser in Berlin during 1913. (*CD/Author*)

Being a boy of spirit, he wouldn't buckle no matter what the pressure, but he did begin to absorb some of the strictly applied lessons, learning the benefits of order and discipline along the way. However, he struggled academically and just managed to graduate in 1909, so he could attend the Prussian Military Academy at Lichterfelde to begin officer training. Here again, he failed to shine academically and had to resit his final exams before being commissioned into the 1st Regiment (Emperor Alexander III) of Uhlans in 1911.

Life in such a regiment in peacetime was similar to being a member of a gentlemen's club. There were parades to attend and military manoeuvres to practice, but this left a lot of time to enjoy life in the mess, riding and hunting. So it is these aspects of army life that tended to engage him, as he recalled in his autobiography:

> My father brought me a beautiful mare called Santuzza. She was a marvellous animal, as hard as nails. She kept her place in a parade like a lamb. In the course of time I discovered that she possessed a great talent for jumping, and I made up my mind to train her. She jumped incredible heights … I hoped to achieve something with her.

This must have been an ideal time for von Richthofen. His duties would not have been too onerous, he had officer status, was free to enjoy countryside pursuits whenever he could and was living close to home, with all the benefits that this could offer. And after attending a massive military parade in Berlin during late 1913, his life must have seemed set fair for a bright future. Yet in the background the pressures that had been building in Europe for a long time finally exploded into a war of unimaginable violence. Although planned long in advance, it still took many by surprise as Manfred, whose regiment was guarding Germany's border near Ostrovo, west of the Prosno River, recalled in 1917:

> For several months all were accustomed to war talk. We had so often packed our service trunks that the whole thing had become tedious. No one believed any longer that there would be war. We who were close to the frontier believed least that there would be a war.
>
> On the day before military operations began we were sitting in the Officers' Club eating oysters, drinking champagne and gambling a little. We were very merry. No one thought of war … Suddenly the door opened. It was Count Kospoth, the administrator. He looked like a ghost and had come to the frontier to convince himself that the rumours of an impending war were true … We learned from him that all the bridges in Silesia were being guarded by the military and that steps were being taken to fortify various positions.
>
> We soon convinced him that the possibility of war was absolutely nil and continued with our festivities. On the next day we were ordered to take to the field.

Faced with a war on two fronts, Germany's strategists had always been aware of the need to crush the French army before Russia's slow-moving mobilisation could take effect. As a result, a rapid advance westward soon followed with only a holding force left in the east to face the enemy there. After some initial skirmishing against the Russians, Manfred's regiment soon joined the thrust through Belgium into France, seeing much action there. By October both sides had begun to dig in and soon a line of trenches stretched from the English Channel to the Swiss border and siege warfare began.

Suddenly there was no need for mounted troops and many cavalrymen, like Manfred, found themselves in the front line living a troglodyte existence as a cold, barren winter approached. He soon baulked at this life and began to look skywards and wondered whether that might be a better place to fight a war:

For some weeks the German army enjoyed great success as it advanced into Belgium and France, but its over reliance on 'footslogging', plus stiffening resistance, eventually drove them to ground. While a war of movement lasted the cavalry could undertake its traditional battlefield role. Manfred is reputed to be the central figure in the lower picture taken in August/September 1914 that graced the front page of the widely read *Illustrierte Unterhaltungs-Beilage*. (*CD/Author*)

For the first few weeks of war the Uhlans found themselves scouting and skirmishing as they had been trained to do. But by October they had been stripped of their horses and found themselves occupying trenches as foot soldiers. For Manfred it proved to be a difficult transition. (*Author*)

(Top) Manfred is reputed to be the officer second from the right in this group photo taken in the Winter of 1914–15, released from the trenches of Verdun for a brief moment. (Bottom) Although appearing dry and well-constructed, trenches were dangerous, uncomfortable places to live and die, with the appalling living conditions causing as many casualties as enemy gunfire. (*CD/Author*)

I am a restless spirit … At the beginning I was in a spot where nothing happened. Then I became a despatch-bearer … The fighting men despised me and considered me a 'Base-hog'. I was not really at the base and I wasn't allowed to advance within 1,500 yards of the front trenches. There below ground I had a bomb-proof, heated abode. Now and then I had to go forward into the front line, which was a great physical exertion. I had to trudge uphill and downhill, criss-cross through an unending number of trenches and mire-holes until at last arriving at a place where men were firing … my position seemed to me a very stupid one.

I had no idea about the activity of our flying men. At any rate, I got tremendously excited whenever I saw an aviator. Of course, I had not the slightest idea whether it was a German or enemy airman … The consequence was that every aeroplane we saw we fired upon.

In his memoirs Manfred doesn't explain why he wanted to become an airman. He simply states that, 'eventually they fulfilled my wish. Thus I joined the Flying Service at the end of May 1915.' Such a momentous decision must have come after a period of thought and discussions with comrades or aviators he may have met, but this we can only surmise. It was left to his mother to describe her son's thoughts on the matter:

(Manfred and I) spoke of this and that, exchanged opinions and arguments, his mature, sensible views always surprised me. Then, standing still in front of me, Manfred said, unexpectedly that 'I am going to join the fliers'. There was something very fine and joyful in his voice, as he spoke. I understood nothing of it and could imagine little, yet I knew that once he had spoken it was already a fact to him and the choice was irrevocably made. I therefore said nothing against it – we would get used to it, in respect of Manfred and in spite of his youth. After that I listened with greater interest, as he told me about what he knew of this new weapon. As we went from the garden into the house, I felt with certainty that a new and great task had taken root within him.

## Part 2

# May 1915 to August 1916

In late May 1915 Manfred travelled to Cologne with twenty-nine other candidates for assessment then to begin training with the Flieger-Ersatz-Abteilung No. 7. With no experience of flying up that point, he may have found himself unsuited to such a life and any aspirations he had could quickly have come to nought. The early signs were not good, as he later recorded:

The next morning at seven o'clock I was to fly for the first time … I was naturally very excited, for I had no idea what it would be like. Everyone whom I had asked about his feelings told a different tale. The night before I went to bed earlier than usual to be thoroughly refreshed … We drove to the airfield and I climbed into an aircraft for the first time. The draught from the propeller was a dreadful nuisance. I found it impossible to make myself understood by the pilot. Everything was carried away by the wind. If I held up a piece of paper it disappeared. My safety helmet slid off. My muffler fell off. My jacket was not sufficiently buttoned up. In short, I felt

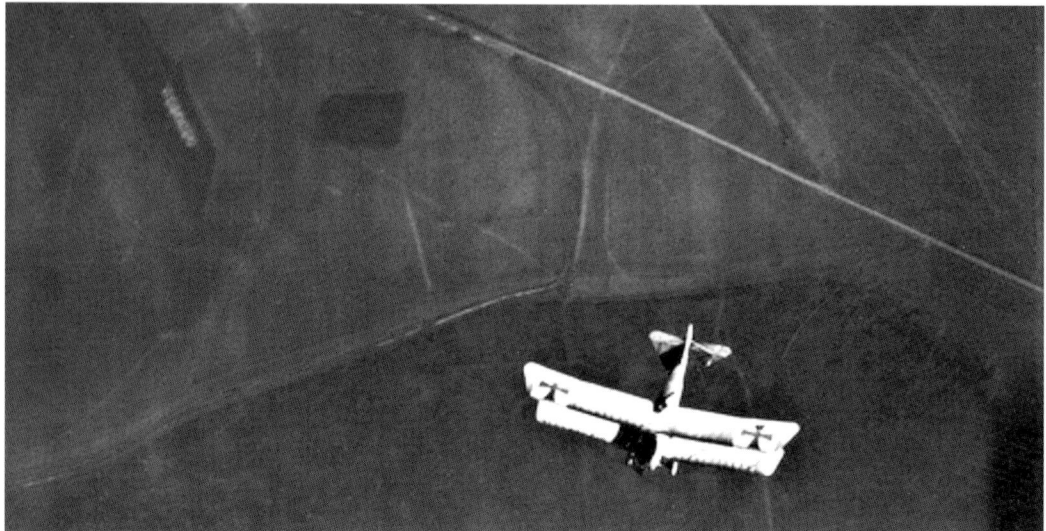

By May 1915, when von Richthofen began training as an observer, the aerial war had advanced considerably with aircraft becoming armed and crews better able to reconnoitre enemy movements and installations more effectively. Combat soon became a regular feature of an aviator's life, though at this stage their aircraft were insufficiently armed to deliver a true killer punch. This would come very soon when fighters began to be fitted with forward-firing machine guns. Here an Albatros two-seater of 1915–16 goes about its business. (*Author*)

very uncomfortable and before I knew what was happening, the pilot accelerated away at full speed ... We went faster and faster. I clutched the sides of the cockpit. Suddenly, the shaking was over and the aircraft was in the air and the earth rapidly dropping away from under me.

As the flight continued he gradually began to settle down, overcoming his initial bewilderment:

I had been told where we were to fly and I was to direct the pilot ... but I lost all sense of direction above our own aerodrome. I had not the slightest idea where I was. I began to look over the side very cautiously at the country ... The houses seemed to have come out from a child's toy box ... Cologne was in the distance, the cathedral looked like a little toy. It was a wonderful feeling to be so high above the earth, to be master of the air. I didn't care a bit where I was, and felt extremely sorry when my pilot thought it was time to descend ... In an aircraft one possesses a feeling of complete security ... At the same time, flying affects one's nerves when racing at full speed through the air, particularly when the aeroplane dips and when the engine stops running and the tremendous noise is followed by an equally tremendous silence ... I counted the hours to my next flight.

Manfred's reaction to this first flight was typical of so many trainee aviators when taking to the air for the first time. But in Manfred's case he soon overcame any nervousness he felt to discover an aptitude for flying and observing, and after a brief period of training was posted to the Eastern Front to join:

The celebrated 69th Squadron [Feldflieger-Abteilung 69 where he would fly Albatros B.II two-seaters]. Being a beginner I felt very foolish. My pilot was a big gun, Oberleutnant Zeumer ... Every day, morning and afternoon, I had to fly and to reconnoitre, and I have brought back valuable information many a time.

During June, July and August I remained with the Flying Service participating in Mackensen's advance from Gorlice to Brest-Litovsk. I had joined as an inexperienced observer and had not the slightest idea about anything ... For an observer it is important to find a pilot with a strong character ... we were told that Count von Holck will join us. Immediately I realised that this is the man for me.

Of his many patrols with both pilots von Richthofen recorded very little, but one patrol stood out in his mind, probably because of von Holck's impetuous nature and great relish in facing danger. They were flying on a reconnaissance mission in the direction of Brest-Litovsk and over Wisznice, which was shrouded in smoke up to a height of 1,800m:

This prevented us from continuing our patrol because we were flying at an altitude of only 1,300 metres ... I advised Holck to fly around the smoke cloud, which would

(Left) Georg Zeumer, who became Manfred's pilot in Feldflieger-Abteilung No. 69 then a very close friend and later helped him qualify as a pilot. In reality, he was suffering with tuberculosis and should have been in hospital, but he was determined to do his duty and did so until killed flying fighters with Jasta 2 on the Western Front on 17 June 1917. (Below) Von Richthofen occasionally formed a partnership in '69' with the 29-year-old Count Carl Friedrich Erich von Holck, a pre-war rider and racing driver of note, who was shot down and killed flying a Fokker Eindecker near St-Rémy on 30 April 1916. Both men clearly had a profound influence on their observer. (*CD*)

have taken about five minutes. Holck did not intend to do this. On the contrary – the greater the danger, the more it attracted him. So, straight through. This nearly cost us dear. As soon as we had disappeared into the smoke the aeroplane began to reel … I couldn't see a thing … Suddenly the machine lost its balance and fell turning, round and round. I managed to grasp a stay and hung onto it, otherwise I would have been thrown out.

We fell down to an altitude of 450 metres over the burning town and suddenly dropped out of the smoke cloud … now we had had enough of it and intended to return … Five minutes later I heard Holck behind me exclaim 'the engine is giving out' and presently it stopped running completely … So we went lower and lower … just managed to glide over a forest and landed at an abandoned artillery position, which the evening before had still been in Russian hands.

We jumped down and rushed into the forest, where we might defend ourselves. When we reached the trees we stopped and I saw a soldier running towards our aircraft … I felt sure he was a Russian. When he came nearer Holck shouted with joy, for he was a Grenadier of the Prussian Guard.

Having survived a very active period of operations, gaining experience and skill in the process, von Richthofen was transferred to the west in May 1915 to join the Brieftauben-Ableitung-Ostende (BAO), where he would be reunited with Georg Zeumer, who had preceded him there:

Zeumer met me at Brussels Station …We were accommodated in a requisitioned hotel on the Ostend Shore and bathed every afternoon. Wrapped up in our many coloured bathing gowns, we sat on the terraces of Ostend and drank our coffee in the afternoon.

It was also at this time that he acquired a companion who would become an important part of his life:

The most beautiful being in all creation is my Danish hound 'Moritz'. I bought him in Ostend for five marks. I was allowed to select one from the litter and chose the prettiest. Zeumer bought another puppy and called him Max.

The BAO was formed in late 1914 to bomb targets in Britain, but at this stage of the war lacked aircraft able to undertake this role effectively. Meanwhile, Zeppelins assumed this offensive role until they became vulnerable to attack from enemy aircraft or gunfire from the ground. By the time von Richthofen joined the unit little had changed and the aviators were making do with an assortment of aircraft for use over the Western Front until they were capable of mounting a bombing campaign against Britain.

On one of these missions, possibly during August, he gave his first 'drop of blood for the Fatherland':

(Top) Von Richthofen relaxing on the beach at Ostend happily puffing a cigar in the early summer of 1915, having joined the Brieftauben-Ableitung-Ostende (BAO) in May (*CD*). (Middle) Von Richthofen's bathing activities were curtailed in September, 'When we suddenly heard bugles and were told that an English Naval Warship Squadron [commanded by Vice-Admiral Reginald Bacon, of the Dover Patrol and consisting of four monitors and an escort] was approaching … We heard a whistling in the air, then a loud explosion as a shell hit that part of the beach where a little earlier we had been bathing. I have never rushed into the "heroes' cellar" as quickly as I did at that moment.' (Bottom) With his close friend Alfred Gerstenberg, possibly from Academy days, who, it seems, he served with in the Uhlans, who then became his observer for a time in Kagohl 2 on the Eastern Front. In August 1917 Gerstenberg joined Manfred in Jasta 11 before being severely wounded three months later. He survived the war and rose to become the *Kommandierender General und Befehlshaber der Deutschen Luftwaffe* in Rumania during 1944 and died of tuberculosis in 1959. (*PC = Pasquale Carisella*)

(Top) Manfred, with his damaged finger still bandaged, poses with fellow officers from the BAO during the late summer of 1915. (Bottom) A photo of AEG G.II No. G6/15 of the BAO, with a black cat emblem on its fuselage, taken at Gistel, inland from Ostend, late in 1915. It is believed that Georg Zeumer, who was nicknamed '*Der Schwarz Katze*', and von Richthofen flew in this slow, unstable aircraft on a number of occasions. (*CD*)

We reached our objective and the first bomb fell. It is interesting to determine its effect – at least one likes to see it explode. Unfortunately, our aircraft had the ridiculous characteristic that one could not see the effect of the bomb because the view was obscured entirely by the wings … Therefore, I signalled to Zeumer that he should turn a little to one side. While waving to him I forgot that the aircraft had two propellers that turned to the right and left of my seat … and bang! my finger was caught. I was a little surprised when I discovered that my little finger had been damaged … I quickly got rid of the rest of my bombs and we hurried home … I had to sit quietly for seven days and was disbarred from flying.

The date 1 September 1915 became a red letter day in von Richthofen's rise to fame:

We flew every day for five and six hours without ever seeing an Englishman. I became increasingly discouraged, but one bright morning we again went out to hunt. Suddenly I saw a Farman aeroplane reconnoitring without taking notice of us. My heart was beating hard when Zeumer flew towards it … Before I knew what was happening we had rushed past each other. I had at most four shots while the Englishman was suddenly behind us firing into our 'shop window' like anything … We turned and turned around one and other until the Englishman, much to our surprise, turned away and flew off. I was greatly disappointed and so was my pilot.

I had always believed that a shot would cause the enemy to fall, but soon realised that an aircraft can stand a great deal of punishment. I felt certain that I would never bring down an enemy aeroplane no matter how much shooting I did.

Charles Donald, from whom this poor-quality negative came, simply wrote that this 'picture shows Manfred in the centre, back to the camera in flying helmet, when serving with the BAO in 1915'. I have no evidence to prove or disprove this, but agree that it is probably von Richthofen. (*CD*)

As air fighting tactics evolved the need for fighters with a gun that could fire through the propeller became of paramount importance. While pilots awaited the development of an effective interrupter gear the French pilot Roland Garros experimented with deflector plates attached to the propeller (top). For a brief time, this 'Heath Robinson' device proved successful and he shot down several aircraft, but its secret was revealed when Garros was forced to land behind enemy lines and taken prisoner on 18 April 1915 (bottom). In this picture he is being interviewed by a number of German officers that day, including, or so Hans-Georg von der Osten believed, von Richthofen (on far right), who, 'told us about this French device, seeing it in operation and meeting the pilot'. Von Richthofen was certainly serving in the Verdun sector at this time so such a meeting cannot be ruled out. (*PC/Author*)

In May–June 1915 Anthony Fokker
took samples of his Fokker Eindecker,
equipped with interrupter gear, to
the Western Front to demonstrate
its capabilities. (Above) Talking to a
group of officers, many of them senior,
about his aircraft. (Right) Dressed in a
German uniform, plus flying goggles,
ostensibly to negate his neutral status as
a Dutchman when flying near or over
the front line. (*CD*)

Lack of experience, plus flying an aircraft not designed for aerial combat, contrived to frustrate them in this endeavour, but they persevered, soon realising that real success could only be found flying single-seater scouts. And in 1915 they did not have to look far to see others benefitting from the development of fighters that could fire through their propeller blades.

First of all, there was the Frenchman Roland Garros, who experimented by fitting protective wedges to the propeller of a Morane-Saulnier parasol monoplane to deflect bullets. Even with this crude arrangement success did not elude him for long. On 1 April 1915 he claimed his first victory when shooting down two Albatros two-seater observation aircraft north of Buc, south-west of Paris, and at least two more enemy aircraft followed later in the month.

The Germans were quick to note all this and wonder what might have been happening to their aircraft. However, fortune soon favoured them when, on 18 April, Garros' aircraft was forced to come down behind enemy lines. Quickly overcome by German troops, he was unable to set fire to his aircraft before being captured, allowing it to be salvaged intact and for its secrets to be revealed. Very quickly the crude but functional method of firing through the propeller was evaluated to see if it might be adapted for use on German aircraft.

As luck would have it, Anthony Fokker, the Dutch aircraft designer and constructor, whose factory lay at Schwerin, had been giving the forward-firing issue some thought before Garros was brought down. Within days, encouraged by Hermann von der Lieth-Thomsen, who had been appointed Chief of Field Air Forces (*Chef des Feldflugwesens*) for the German army in March 1915, Fokker completed the development of an interrupter gear, assisted by Heinrich Lübbe, the watchmaker and engineer, and other members of his team. This was fitted to a Fokker M.5K monoplane, which Fokker demonstrated successfully to staff officers at Döberitz, to the west of Berlin. He was asked to take this invention to France, where it could be shown to front-line officers. By then LMG.08 machine guns had been similarly fitted to the Fokker's E.2.15 and E.3.15 and it was these two aircraft that he took with him to the battlefield for test purposes, plus a converted Fokker A.111 belonging to Leutnant Otto Parschau, which was fitted with a Parabellum machine gun (MG 14) and interrupter gear.

Acceptance soon followed and by July 1915 the Eindecker was beginning to reach the front in sufficient numbers to cause Allied airmen some concern and provide propagandists with new heroes to proclaim and exploit. In the months that followed their domination grew, as did the reputations of the pilots, Oswald Boelcke in particular. By October he had shot down six enemy aircraft and nineteen by June 1916, when he was rested from front-line service. Along the way he was awarded the Pour le Mérite and became a national idol feted by the press and pursued by admirers. Von Richthofen must have observed all this happening and been greatly encouraged in his ambition to become a pilot. However, for the moment, he remained an observer seeking combat whenever he could and in the Champagne region that autumn, where his unit was operating that month, he tasted blood for the first time:

Leutnant Parschau †

wegen hervorragender Leistungen als Kampfflieger durch die Verleihung des Ordens „Pour le Mérite" ausgezeichnet.
Nach photographischer Aufnahme.

During 1915 the cult of the fighter ace was born as the Fokker Eindeckers began to dominate the skies over the Western Front. These men proved a godsend to the German propaganda machine and received wide, and probably unwanted, publicity. But celebrating their hero status in such a graphic way came with an obvious flaw – death could easily intervene, as it did in these three cases. (Top left to right) Otto Parschau, who was killed in action on 21 July 1916; Oswald Boelcke, with a lady friend, who died in a collision with a comrade on 28 October 1916; and (below) Max Immelmann, who was shot down and killed on 18 June 1916. This constant haemorrhage of aces drove the need to find new heroes and in von Richthofen they found the supreme example to exploit. (CD/PC)

(Top) Oswald Boelcke in flying rig, standing in front of a Fokker E.IV Eindecker. (Bottom) According to Charles Donald's notes, Boelcke revs the engine of his Fokker Eindecker prior to take-off at Sivry in 1916. (*CD*)

I flew with (Oberleutnant Paul) von Osterroht, who had a smaller aircraft than the 'apple-barge' [type unknown]. About three miles behind the enemy lines we came across a Farman two-seater. He allowed us to approach him, and for the first-time I saw an aerial opponent at close quarters. Osterroht flew with great skill, so I could easily fire at the enemy. Our opponent probably did not notice us, for only when I had trouble with my gun did he begin to shoot back at us.

When my supply of 100 cartridges had been used I suddenly noticed the Farman going down in peculiar spirals. I followed him with my eyes and tapped Osterroht on the head to draw his attention. Our opponent fell and fell and finally crashed into a large crater. There he stood on his nose, the tail pointing to the sky. According to my map, he had fallen three miles behind the front … At the time no notice was taken of aeroplanes brought down in enemy territory, otherwise I should have one more aeroplane to my credit.

Perhaps more importantly von Richthofen had recently met Boelcke for the first time, when traveling by the same train to Rethel:

In the dining car at the table next to me was a young, unimposing-looking leutnant. There was no need to take any notice of him except for the fact that he was the only man who had succeeded in shooting down hostile aircraft, not once but four times. His name has been mentioned in communiques. I thought much of him because of what he was achieving. Although I had tried hard I had not brought an enemy down up to that time.

I wanted to find out how Leutnant Boelcke managed this business. So I asked him 'how to you do it?'. He seemed amused and laughed, although I had asked him quite seriously. Then he replied that, 'It is quite simple. I fly close to my man, aim well and then, of course, he goes down.' I shook my head and told him that I did the same, but my opponent, unfortunately, did not go down. The difference between us was he flew a Fokker and I a large aircraft.

I took the trouble to get more closely acquainted with this nice, modest man, whom I desperately wanted to teach me this business We often played cards together, went for walks and I asked him many questions. Finally, I decided that I would also learn to fly a Fokker. Perhaps then my luck would improve. From then on my whole objective and ambition was focussed on learning to manipulate the stick myself … Happily, I soon found an opportunity to learn piloting on an 'old box' in the Champagne.

In his eagerness to learn to fly Manfred persuaded Georg Zeumer to give him a few unofficial lessons in an effort to acquire some basic flying skills. After a little more than a week of practice flying Zeumer allowed his observer to fly solo, presumably hoping that this might satisfy von Richthofen's immediate demands. Inevitably, things went badly:

I started off, the aircraft reached the prescribed speed and I couldn't help noticing that I was actually flying. I didn't feel nervous, but elated … I made a wide turn to the left, cut the engine exactly where I had been ordered to do so and prepared for what should happen next. Now came the most difficult part – the landing. I remembered exactly what I had to do. I acted automatically, but the aircraft moved quite differently from the way I expected. I lost my sense of balance and made some wrong movements and stood the aircraft on its nose and succeeded in turning my aeroplane into a battered 'school bus'.

Having escaped injury by a hairbreadth, one might have expected Manfred to take things more slowly, but instead he 'went with great passion at flying and suddenly I could handle the aircraft'. But before he could become a pilot he had to pass three increasingly difficult exams if he were to be awarded his pilot's badge. In mid-October 1915 he undertook the first test locally under the critical eye of the renowned aviator Hauptmann Rudolf von Thuna, who was the air services inspecting officer. Having carefully observed von Richthofen fly a figures of eight several times and then land, he found insufficient evidence of competence to pass him. Not deterred, Manfred practised more and sought re-examination. At the same time, perhaps realising that he needed more instruction, he submitted an application to train as a pilot at Fliegerschule (flight school), where he would meet von Thuna again and be instructed by him.

When recalling this crucial stage on his path to becoming a pilot, Manfred simply recorded that:

I went through my training with a dear fellow, Oberleutnant Bodo von Lyncker … our aim was to fly Fokkers with a Fighting Squadron on the Western Front … On Christmas day I passed my third examination. In connection with this I flew to Schwerin where the Fokker works are based and from there flew to Breslau, Schweidnitz and Luben before returning to Berlin. During my tour I landed in lots of different places, visiting relatives and friends along the way.

After this brief tour of his homeland, Manfred was awarded his pilot's badge in early 1916. In the intervening years it has been said that he wasn't a skilled pilot. This may well be true, but Anthony Fokker, who saw him in action and knew what made a good combat pilot, has offered us a more studied view of von Richthofen's flying abilities:

Without the instinctive skills which Boelcke and Immelmann possessed, von Richthofen was slow to learn to fly, crashing on his first solo and only mastering the aircraft by sheer force of personality. Time and again he escaped death by a miracle before he managed to conquer the 'unruly' aeroplane … Ultimately he became an excellent flyer, but whereas many other pilots flew with a kind of innocent courage, Richthofen flew with his brains and made his ability serve him.

Learning to fly in the early years of the war could be a hit or miss affair, with a slowly evolving training schedule that failed to keep casualties to a minimum. Von Richthofen was given ad hoc lessons by his pilot, Georg Zeumer, before coming under the control of the famous pre-war aviator Rudolf von Thuna, by then the inspecting officer for training (top photo in the centre facing the camera). (Middle) To help trainees get to grips with firing guns, this contraption was built that could be wheeled around, allowing its 'pilot' to line up on targets and shoot. It is said that von Richthofen is the man second from the right. (Bottom) Ground control of trainees while flying was a simple affair, with hand signs and flags being the sole means of communication. (*CD/Author*)

After kicking his heels in Germany for nearly three months, von Richthofen returned to the front in mid-March 1916 and was assigned to Kasta 8 of Kagohl 2, commanded by Hauptmann Victor Carganico, based at an airfield near Landres, to the north-east of Verdun. On its strength at the time, and likely to have attracted Manfred's attention, were a small number of Fokker Eindeckers. However, his arrival seems to have coincided with these aircraft being gathered together into two special fighter units, known as Kampfeinsitzer Kommandos (KEKs), leaving Kasta 8 as a two-seater squadron only. However, any disappointment he felt might have been assuaged by the allocation of a few more fighters to the Kastas as production rates improved. In the meantime, he flew the LVG C.II and then the faster Roland C.II Walfisch. Despite being quite cumbersome aircraft in comparison to fighters, von Richthofen continued to seek combat when he could:

A scene very familiar to von Richthofen in the summer of 1916 during the Battle for Verdun – the badly damaged Fort Douaumont and surrounding trenches that lay at the centre of German efforts to overcome the French. This bloody contest was one of little movement and great slaughter, with only the airmen ever clearly seeing what was happening on the ground. It was here that von Richthofen regularly sought combat and tried to hone his skills. (*Author*)

In the official communique of 26th April I achieved a citation for the first time, although I was not mentioned by name – only my accomplishment appeared. I had a machine gun which I had mounted in the same way as found on Nieuport machines [if so it was positioned on the top wing and so fired outside the arc of the propeller]. People laughed at the way I had it fitted because the whole thing looked so primitive. Of course, I swore by this arrangement, and very soon I had the opportunity of assessing its value in practice.

I encountered a hostile Nieuport aircraft apparently flown by a man who was also a beginner, for he acted very stupidly. When I flew towards him he flew away – apparently experiencing trouble with his gun. I had no idea how to tackle him, but thought, 'What will happen if I simply start shooting at him?' So, I flew after him, approaching as close as possible and began firing a short series of bursts with my gun. The Nieuport reared up and turned over and over.

At first my observer and I believed this was a ruse but the machine went lower and lower. Finally, my observer patted me on the head and called out, 'I congratulate you. He is falling'. As a matter of fact he fell into a forest behind Fort Douaumont and disappeared in the trees … behind enemy lines. I flew home and merely reported that, 'I had an aerial fight and have shot down a Nieuport.' Next day I read of my action in the communique.

Von Richthofen when serving with Jasta 2 and seen talking to his 29-year-old commanding officer, Hauptmann Victor Carganico. The CO survived the war to join the post-war Luftwaffe and rise to the rank of major general. His son, Horst, became a sixty-victory ace in the Second World War, before being killed in May 1944. His father survived him by a year, seemingly being executed by Russian soldiers at Gut Neugrimnitz on 27 May 1945. (*CD*)

(Top) Roland C.II Walfisch of Kasta 8 before transferring to the Eastern Front. It has been said that von Richthofen and Alfred Gerstenberg are sitting atop of the aircraft on the extreme left. (Bottom) Charles Donald has written on the back of this photograph 'Kasts 8 – a typical scene in the Summer of 1916 before transferring to the Eastern Front. MvR stands in front of the Fokker EIII'. True or not, this picture does at least capture life on a squadron at this time of war. (*CD*)

By this stage a Fokker Eindecker had been allocated to No. 8, which gave von Richthofen his chance to fly a fighter in combat for the first time:

> After canvassing my commanding officer for some time I was at last given permission to fly a Fokker. The rotating engine was a novelty and it was a strange feeling to be quite alone during a flight. This aircraft jointly belonged to a friend of mine (Leutnant Hans Reimann) and myself. Both he and I were afraid that the other would smash up the 'box'.

Reimann, who was the first to try the Fokker, took it up and fought with a Nieuport scout, which forced him to crash land between the lines, from where he made good his escape. Luckily, a replacement Fokker soon arrived and it was von Richthofen's turn to test his mettle, but he didn't have an auspicious start:

This time I felt a moral obligation to attend to its destruction myself! I was flying for the third time when the engine suddenly stopped running. I had to land right away in a field and, in a moment, this beautiful machine was converted into a mass of scrap metal. It was a miracle that I was not hurt.

With no more fighters forthcoming, both men had to be satisfied with going to war in two-seaters, this time to bolster the army on the Eastern Front. Here intelligence gathering gradually revealed that the Russians were massing for an attack, with the aim of drawing fire away from that summer's 'Big Push' on the Somme. With German forces in increasing danger on two fronts, but weaker in the east, reinforcements were soon being despatched to counter the threat there. Increased reconnaissance was essential and the battle-hardened Kagohl 2 was soon on their way to provide this support.

After a four-day journey, Manfred arrived in north-western Ukraine on 1 July to begin operations. However, it was a tour of duty destined to last for only two months, brought to an end by Oswald Boelcke's intervention. In the meantime, Manfred was fully involved in the new campaign:

At last we arrived at Kovel, where we remained accommodated in our railway carriages. There are many advantages in dwelling in a train. One is that we are

Having seen Hans Reimann lose Kasta 8s only Fokker Eindecker, von Richthofen quickly demolished its replacement – though probably bore no responsibility for the engine failure that led to the crash. He seems to have escaped injury, though the plane was wrecked. His dog, Moritz, and members of the Kasta pose beside the aircraft's remains. (*CD*)

(Top) A group photo apparently taken at Lesnaya in the summer. Von Richthofen stands in the very back row second from the right, while Gerstenberg is in the front row on the far right. (Below) Under inspection by Prince Leopold of Bavaria, who commanded the 9th Army on the Eastern Front, a photo most probably taken in July 1916. Von Richthofen is immediately in front of the prince with Alfred Gerstenberg to his right. (*CD*)

always ready to travel and need not change our quarters. However, in the heat of the Russian summer a sleeping car is unbearable. Therefore, I agreed with my friends Gerstenberg and Franz Christian von Scheele to 'take quarters' in the forest nearby.

The attacks went on day after day with little way of knowing what damage they were doing or if their efforts were worthwhile. The daytime temperatures in the vastness of Ukraine during August can reach unbearable heights and so it proved to be that summer. There was little to do between raids except sit about trying to find whatever shade they could, anything unusual happening to relieve the boredom being greatly valued. A visit by Boelcke provided just the tonic they needed:

In the evening the great man duly arrived … He imagined that he would now go to the Somme to organise a new fighting squadron (Jagdstaffel 2). He had been authorised to choose men who seemed particularly well-qualified for this purpose.

I dared not ask him to be taken on … Still the idea of fighting again on the Western Front appealed to me. There is nothing finer for a young cavalry officer than a chase in the air.

The next morning, he was to leave us. Quite early somebody knocked on my door and before me stood the great man with his Pour le Mérite … I had never imagined that he had come to look me up in order to ask me to become his pupil. I almost fell on his neck when he asked me whether I cared to go with him to the Somme. Three days later I was on a railway train travelling through the whole of Germany straight to my new squadron. At last my greatest wish was fulfilled.

When I left a good friend of mine called out after me, 'Don't come back without the Pour le Mérite.'

Within days Manfred was heading westwards to begin life as a fighter pilot with Jasta 2 little knowing what lay in store or the fame that awaited him.

# Part 3

# September 1916 to March 1917

By the time von Richthofen arrived in France the Battle of the Somme was reaching its violent conclusion. Since July the British and French armies had been pummelling the enemy lines with little success and the most appalling losses. The cost in casualties is generally accepted to have exceeded 1 million men and the ground gained minimal. Yet the Allies persisted and in September were still trying to take enemy positions that should, if their strategies and tactics had been sound, have been overrun in July. Looking down from on high, Manfred would have observed all this and begun to play his part in the continuing slaughter.

Shortly after Jasta 2 was established in August aircraft began to arrive. Vizefeldwebel Leopold Reimann brought a single Albatros with him from Jasta 1 and shortly afterwards two new Fokker D.III biplanes were flown in from 2nd Army's air park. And it was in one of these two aircraft that Boelcke forced down his twentieth victim on 2 September over Thiepval – a DH.2 flown by Captain Robert Wilson.

As the days passed other new pilots began to arrive, including von Richthofen, who soon began to absorb many valuable lessons imparted by his leader, Boelcke. Key among them was the need to fly as a co-ordinated group and the need to secure an advantage by using speed and height. Then there were such specific things as choosing when and where to attack and then open fire, making use of the weather conditions to screen an approach – out of the sun if possible – and much more. However, theory has to be turned into practice at some point and on 17 September 1916 Manfred did just so, as he later reported:

On the previous day we received our new aeroplanes, and the next day (the 17th September) Boelcke was to fly with us. We were all beginners, so everything he said to us was important and entirely true.

The 17th was a gloriously fine day, so it was to be expected that the English would be very active. Before we set off Boelcke repeated his instructions and for the first time we flew as a squadron … We had just arrived at the front when we saw an enemy squadron proceeding towards Cambrai. Of course, Boelcke saw them first … Soon we understood the situation, and we all endeavoured to follow Boelcke very closely.

We approached cautiously and positioned ourselves between the front and our opponents. If they wished to turn back, they had to pass us first … They were seven in number and we were only five. All the Englishmen flew large bomb-carrying two seaters and in a few seconds the 'dance' began.

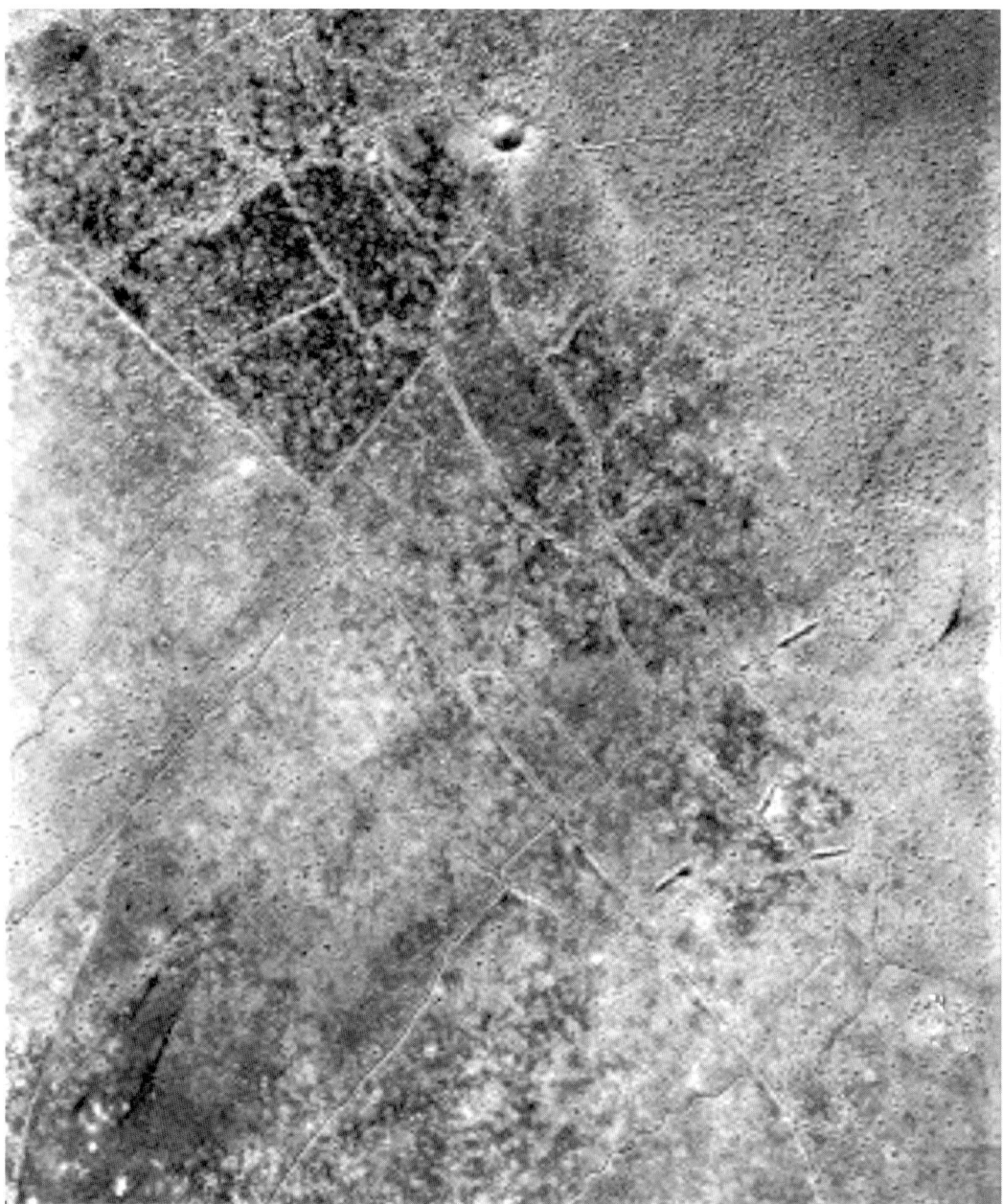

Some historians consider the Battle of the Somme in 1916 to be the bloodiest confrontation of the Great War. True or not, the four months in which it raged inflicted the most appalling losses on both sides of the lines and earth-shattering barrages churned up a vast area of land (above). It was over this scene of devastation that von Richthofen fought and established his reputation with Oswald Boelcke and Jasta 2 in the last few months of that year. (*Author*)

Boelcke (centre) smiling for the camera shortly after Jasta 2 was formed, according to notes that came with this photograph. Von Richthofen stands on the left with his back to the photographer, while a group of British and Empire prisoners of war look on. Some are smiling – probably glad to be away from the slaughterhouse. (*CD*)

Late 1916 and von Richthofen sits with fellow Jasta 2 officers scanning the sky over the Western Front with binoculars hoping to see signs of enemy activity. (*CD*)

Typical scenes showing the cycle of activity each day in Jasta 2 at Bertincourt and Lagnicourt. (Top) Von Richthofen poses in what may be his Albatros D.II. The remainder of the photos show the Jasta before and after operational flights. The two lower pictures on the adjoining page demonstrate how the young pilots, including Manfred, gathered around Boelcke when he returned from a mission hanging on his every word eager to hear how he it went and with what success. In the weeks before his death on 28 October 1916 he would shoot down twenty more aircraft, raising his list of victories to forty. In the bottom photo the 'master' wipes his face to remove the grime of battle, Manfred in attendance. (*CD/Author*)

Boelcke closed in on the first enemy machine, but did not shoot. I followed, with my comrades close by … I did not think for long and took aim and fired as he shot back. We both missed and a struggle began. It was important for me to get on his tail … Apparently he was no beginner, because he knew it would be the end if I got behind him. At this time I did not have the belief that 'he must fall' in these situations, but on this occasion I was just curious to see whether he would go down. There is a great difference between these two feelings. When you have shot down your first, second or third opponent then one begins to understand how it is done.

My enemy twisted and turned, flying in zigzag way. I am driven by a single thought, 'he must go down whatever happens'. At last, a favourable moment arrives when he has apparently lost sight of me. Instead of twisting and turning he flies straight and level. In a fraction of a second I am on his tail … I fire a short burst … I had flown so close I thought I might crash into him. Suddenly I yelled with excitement, the propeller had stopped turning and he was forced to land and it was impossible for him to reach his own lines. The aircraft was swinging from side to side. Probably something had happened to the pilot and the observer was no longer visible.

The Englishman landed close to the airfield of one of our squadrons. I was so excited that I landed also. In my eagerness I nearly smashed up my machine … I rushed over and saw a lot of soldiers were running towards the enemy. When I arrived, I discovered that I had in fact shot the engine to pieces, and the pilot and observer were severely wounded. The observer died at once and the pilot while being taken to the nearest dressing station. I honoured the fallen enemy by placing a stone on their grave.

When I returned to base, Boelcke and my other comrades were already at breakfast … I proudly reported that I had shot down an Englishman. All were elated, for I was not the only one who had been victorious.

Von Richthofen's first victory on 17 September 1916, an F.E.2b from 11 Squadron flown by Lionel Morris and Tom Rees, both of whom died of their wounds. (*CD*)

Flushed with success, von Richthofen settled into the routine of flying the single-seater fighters. There would be many frustrating days as he continued learning this craft. Yet, at the same time, he would look on in admiration, and perhaps some envy, as his leader went up almost daily to seek the enemy, rapidly extending his list of victims:

> This was a time when Boelcke's 'bag' of aircraft shot down increased from twenty to forty within two months. We beginners had not, at the time, his experience, and were satisfied when we did not get a hiding. It was a wonderful phase. Every time we went up we had a fight. Frequently we fought really big battles with forty to sixty English aircraft and unfortunately were often in the minority … Sometimes they came down to a very low level and visited Boelcke in his quarters, at which they threw their bombs … The spirit of our leader inspired all his pupils. We trusted him blindly.

Slowly but surely, as the Battle of the Somme drew to a close, and the pressure began to ease a little bit, the number of aircraft von Richthofen shot down grew. Two went down to his guns on 23 and 30 September 1916, then four more in October, but a tragedy lay in store that would have very serious consequences for the squadron and a much wider audience.

Following an enemy raid on Bertincourt it was decided to transfer Jasta 2 to Lagnicourt, so slightly further away from the front line. At the time Boelcke was almost crippled by severe attacks of asthma and should have been hospitalised, but he refused to leave his squadron, later writing that:

> I have to give my pilots some training. That is not so simple because they are all inspired with such fiery zeal that it is often difficult to put the brakes on them …

Boelcke stands next to a captured DH.2 chatting to von Richthofen in the cockpit, presumably assessing the capabilities of the pusher biplane. (*CD*)

But until I get it into their heads that everything depends on sticking together through thick and thin and that it doesn't matter who actually registers a victory as long as the Staffel wins … I can talk myself silly, and sometimes I have to turn my heavy batteries on them … But they take it very willingly.

However, on 28 October, and still in the throes of asthmatic attacks, this lack of co-ordination may have to contributed to Boelcke's death, as von Richthofen related:

We were flying once more led by Boelcke. The weather was gusty with many clouds.

From a long way away we saw two Englishmen in the air … We were six … The fight began in the usual way. Boelcke tackled one and I the other. I had to break away because a German machine got in my way. I looked around and noticed Boelcke getting on the tail of his victim 180 metres away from me … Close to Boelcke flew a good friend of his (Erwin Bohme) … both men were shooting and it was likely that the Englishman would fall at any moment. Suddenly I saw the two German machines make a wrong move. Immediately I thought, 'collision'. The two aircraft merely touched one another … Boelcke drew away from his victim and descended in wide curves … Now his aircraft was no longer controllable. It fell accompanied by his faithful friend.

A wing broke off and he plunged into the ground. His skull was fractured in the impact, so he was dead at once. It affected us all deeply, as if one of our favourite brothers had been taken. At his funeral, I carried the pillow with his medals. In six weeks we have had six dead and one wounded: two have lost their nerve.

Very quickly after Boelcke's death Stephan Kirmaier was promoted to Oberleutnant and placed in command of the Jasta, successfully leading the squadron until himself killed during November 1916, having brought down enemy aircraft on eleven occasions. His going left a gap that was temporarily filled by the Jasta's non-flying chief administrative officer, Oberleutnant Karl-Heinrich Bodenschatz, a man who would soon become an important figure in Manfred's life. While this happened it was necessary for a senior pilot to oversee operational matters and von Richthofen fulfilled this role until a permanent replacement was found. This proved to be Oberleutnant Franz Walz, a pre-war aviator who, when flying two-seater reconnaissance aircraft, had been credited with six victories. Having just overseen the creation of Jasta 19, he was thought to be a sound replacement for Kirmaier. However, he seems to have lacked the fighting spirit of his two predecessors or von Richthofen, who probably still continued to play a leading role in the air as his star continued to rise.

In the weeks that followed von Richthofen continued to ply his trade with ever increasing success, mostly downing British two-seater observation aircraft. Then on 23 November he met a British 'ace' who could be more than a match for him. It was an event of such importance that it would draw even more attention to von Richthofen and help

28 October 1916 and Boelcke's last day. (Top) A photo reputed to have been taken immediately prior to his last mission, the results of which are captured in the other two pictures. After a collision with fellow pilot Erwin Bohme his aircraft shed part of its upper wing, which then became uncontrollable and crashed. Boelcke's head was crushed on impact, presumably killing him instantly. (*CD/PC*)

(Top) To allow Boelcke's body to displayed in an open casket, his badly damaged skull had to be rebuilt by the medics and then made up by the undertakers to make the corpse presentable. (Lower) Von Richthofen was chosen to carry Boelcke's many decorations behind the coffin and is seen here before and after the ceremony at Cambrai on the 31 October 1916. (*CD/Author*)

As von Richthofen settled into his stride with Jasta 2, and achieved success as a fighter pilot, he soon began to exude the assurance of a veteran. This photo, taken in the autumn of 1916, seems to capture this growing self-awareness and presents a picture of someone capable of leading others. If so, he had learned much from Boelcke in a very short time. (*CD*)

By the end of 1916 the pusher DH.2 fighter was outpaced and outclassed by the Albatros D.II and even in the hands of an experienced pilot struggled for survival. On 23 November von Richthofen met Major Lanoe Hawker VC, a leading British ace and commanding officer of 24 Squadron, in combat and even with all his hard-earned skill the Englishman did not survive the encounter. (*Author*)

Major Hawker, like von Richthofen would shortly become, was a national hero who attracted many headlines. (Below) After a long struggle with von Richthofen he was shot down and buried by German soldiers beside his aircraft – a makeshift cross being placed over his grave. With the battle still raging around the wreck, his grave and the remains of his aircraft were soon obliterated. (*CD/Author*)

GALLIPOLI HEROES PICK THEIR OWN V.C.s.

# DAILY SKETCH.

GUARANTEED DAILY NETT SALE MORE THAN 1,000,000 COPIES.

THE V.C. WHO ROUTED THREE GERMAN AIRMEN.

promote his cause even more, as Germany's High Command sought to create new heroes for public consumption.

In his memoirs von Richthofen simply wrote 'Major Hawker' before describing this noteworthy day:

> I noticed three Englishmen … I felt strongly inclined to fight … I was flying at a lower altitude and waited until one of the enemy aircraft tried to drop on me.

A little later one came 'sailing along' and wanted to tackle me from behind. After firing five shots he had to break away, as I swerved into a tight turn. He tried to catch me up from behind, as I tried to get on his tail. So we circled round and round each other like madmen at a height of 3,000 metres.

First we turned twenty times to the left, and then thirty times to the right, each trying to get behind and above the other. I soon realised I was not fighting a beginner and had not the slightest intention of breaking away. He was flying in a 'box' that could turn superbly. However, my 'packing case' was better at climbing than his and I, at last, succeeded in getting above and behind my English waltzing partner.

When we were down to about 1,800 metres, without having achieved anything in particular, my opponent should have realised that it was the time to leave. The wind was in my favour and was driving us further over our side of the lines. But this gallant man was full of courage and when we were down to 900 metres he cheerfully waved to me as if to say 'Well, how do you do?'

The circles we made around each other were now so small that their diameter was probably no more than 75 to 90 metres … I looked down into his aircraft and could see every movement of his head. If he had not been wearing a helmet I would have been able to see the expressions he was making.

He was a good sportsman but by and by things became a little too hot for him. He had to decide whether to land on German ground or fly back to the English lines. He tried the latter, after trying in vain to escape me by looping and such manoeuvres … He went down to 90 metres and tried to escape by flying a zig-zag course … This was my most advantageous moment. I followed him at a height of 75 to 45 metres, firing all the time, but my guns jammed and nearly robbed me of my success.

However, my opponent crashed, having been shot through the head, 45 metres inside our lines. His machine gun was dug out of the ground and now graces the entrance of my dwelling.

I was extremely proud when I was informed that the aviator I had brought down on 23 November 1916 was the English Immelmann. In view of the nature of the battle it was clear to me that I had fought a flying ace.

Lanoe Hawker, a 25-year-old Englishman and fighter ace of note, was worthy of this praise, having become a well-established fighter pilot and been awarded the Victoria Cross when showing great courage on 25 July 1915 when single-handedly driving down three German aircraft. Such was his reputation that word of his gallantry and accomplishments had spread to the German side of the lines. In the circumstances, it is little wonder that von Richthofen felt moved to call him the English Immelmann.

Manfred spent Christmas that year with Jasta 2, being joined there by his father and brother for the celebrations. In a letter to his mother on 28 December 1916, he described this brief pause in the action:

Jasta 2's pilots in the autumn of 1916, von Richthofen third from the left. Charles Donald believed this picture to have been taken in September, but other sources place it later, in November, by which time Oberleutnant Kirmaier (centre) had succeeded Oswald Boelcke as Staffelführer. (*CD*)

Albrecht von Richthofen (seated enjoying a cigar) enjoys the company of his sons (behind him to left and right) and the other pilots of Jasta 2 (now renamed Jasta Boelcke) at Christmas 1916. (*Author*)

Papa and Lothar both joined me on Christmas Eve. It was a memorable day. Christmas in the field was indeed more fun than you in the homeland might think. Our celebrations consisted of a Christmas tree and a very good meal. The next day, Lothar made his first solo flight. A comparable event will be his first victory. Yesterday I shot down my 15th Englishman …

In recognition of his success Manfred was promoted to command Jasta 11 on 15 January 1917 and, a day later, received word that he had been awarded the Pour le Mérite by the Kaiser on 12 January.

Formed in October 1916, the squadron had first been led by the experienced 27-year-old Oberleutnant Rudolf Emil Lang, who had trained as an aviator during 1914. Various postings then followed, during which Lang seems to have flown two-seater reconnaissance aircraft for the most part. In December 1915 he was posted to FFA 6b to fly a Fokker or Pfalz monoplane, and then in May 1916 he transferred to Artillerie-Fliegerabteilung 103b, remaining there for only two months until placed in command of Kampfstaffel 31b. With such a wealth of experience he must have seemed a wise choice to lead Jasta 11, but success in this role eluded him.

It has been suggested that he was ill-suited to command a fighter squadron, lacked the skill to train his men as Boelcke had done and did not display sufficient fighting spirit, leaving his pilots leaderless where it mattered most – in the air. True or not, by Christmas the Jasta had claimed only one victory, by Leutnant Konstantin Krefft, which

This photograph is thought to have been taken early in 1917 shortly after von Richthofen had taken over Jasta 11 and was visiting Flieger-Abteilung No. 258 in his Albatros D.III. His old friend Prince Friedrich Karl of Prussia was commanding officer of 258, a reconnaissance and artillery spotting squadron, but was personally allocated an Albatros D.I, emblazoned with the Hussar's death's head insignia, which he flew occasionally, or so it seems, with Jasta 2. This aircraft, in which Prince Friedrich was forced down in no man's land on 21 March 1917, then shot trying to escape, dying of his wounds on 6 April, is to the right. (*CD*)

A photograph that appeared in the German press during March 1917 showing von Richthofen in his 'furs', presumably having returned from a recent flight. The other officer is not recorded, nor is the meaning of the number 92 in the background. By March von Richthofen's name was becoming much more well-known and his rise to national fame well under way. (*Author*)

had not been confirmed. They were floundering and their lack of success undoubtedly attracted criticism, which quickly benefited von Richthofen. He replaced Lang, who was transferred to Jasta 28 to try again.

It remained to be seen if von Richthofen could do any better, but he began his command in a positive way by flying a new Albatros D.III from Pronville to La Brayelle, suggesting that a strong new leader, suitably armed, had arrived. Up to then the Jasta seems to have made do with Halberstadt D.II and D.Vs and a few Albatros D.Is, which may have contributed to their lack of success. Over the next few weeks this changed quickly as von Richthofen led his pilots to greater success.

A photograph purported to show von Richthofen's Albatros D.III on 24 January 1917 after its wing failure that day when attacking an F.E.2b of 25 Squadron. He was very lucky to have reached the ground safely, something that was unlikely to have happened if the top wing had failed as catastrophically. (*CD*)

Although Jasta 11 had under-achieved until he arrived, the basic material he inherited, and would then add to, proved to be quite promising. In due course two of the pilots, Karl Allmenröder and Kurt Wolff, would become leading aces and Pour le Mérite holders, and two others he enlisted later on, Karl Emil Schäfer and his brother Lothar, would do likewise. Added to this there were a few others, like Bockelmann, Esser, Mohnicke and Festner, who would also do well under his leadership.

Manfred may also have been helped in his great endeavour by the arrival of the Albatros D.IIIs. Not only were they the best available, but their sleek looks held greater aesthetic appeal for the men destined to fly them. These things shouldn't matter, but they often do, especially to the young who are often image conscious. But to this touch of vanity von Richthofen soon added a embellishment of his own – having his aircraft painted red overall. At a time when propagandists were keenly developing the hero cult, such a development was bound to be seized upon and so the *Der Rote Kampfflieger* was born. It was an image that soon spread to the other side of the lines, as he later reported:

I had the good fortune to shoot at a Vickers two seater [an F.E.2b on 24 January 1917 for his eighteenth confirmed victory, the seventeenth being claimed on the 23 January] which was peacefully photographing our artillery positions. My friend the photographer did not have the time to defend himself. They had to make haste to get down on to firm land as the aircraft began to give an indication of catching on fire … (and) coming to earth it burst into flames.

I felt pity for them and decided not to send them down, but merely compel them to land … I had the feeling that my opponent was wounded, for he did not fire a single shot.

When down to an altitude of about 500 metres engine trouble compelled me to land without manoeuvring. The result was very comical. My enemy with his burning aircraft landed smoothly, while I, his conqueror, came down beside him in the barbed wire of our trenches and overturned my machine.

The two Englishmen [Lieutenant John MacLennan and Captain Oscar Greig of No. 25 Squadron, both of whom were wounded], who were rather surprised at my crash landing, greeted me like sportsmen … they could not understand why I landed so clumsily.

They were the first Englishmen I had brought down alive, consequently it gave me particular pleasure to talk to them. I asked them whether they had previously seen my machine in the air. One of them replied, 'Oh yes. I know your aircraft very well. We call it "*Le Petit Rouge*"'.

When intercepting MacLennan and Greig on 24 January von Richthofen was forced to land not by engine trouble, as he recorded, but because 'one of my wings broke during the battle … It was only due to a miracle that I reached the ground without being killed. On the same day three new aeroplanes of Jasta Boelcke fell … It is possible that what happened to me happened to them.'

Armed with such graphic evidence of poor design or construction, von Richthofen soon expressed his concerns to those in authority. As a result, the D.IIIs were grounded by the commanding general's staff on 27 January and temporarily replaced by Halberstadts. Suitably modified, the D.IIIs soon returned, but their reputation had been damaged and trust in these aircraft undoubtedly took time to be restored.

With the onset of winter, activity over the front was limited by heavy rain, thick low-lying cloud interspersed with periods of extremely cold, snowy conditions. Although Jasta 11 continued to fly and fight it did so only when the weather allowed and that winter this proved more difficult than usual. One account written by my grandfather, Rifleman Arthur Hillier of the Post Office Rifles, who had served on the Western Front since early 1915, reported that the winter months of 1916–17, 'were almost unbearable in the trenches and, I believe, were by far the worst of the war when it came to the cold and wet. Also by then the pace of war was so hot that rarely was there a "quiet" time when you weren't being shelled. Every night was lit up by gunfire and casualties on both sides were heavy even when there were no pitched battles being fought.'

At least pilots on both sides could escape these appalling conditions between missions, but when in the air, flying at 2,000m or more, the cold could be unbearable despite the crude forms of protective clothing available to them. Nevertheless, when the weather

For the early months of von Richthofen's tenure as Jasta 11's commanding officer the squadron was based at La Brayelle, 3km west of Douai, where these two photos were taken. (Top) It has been suggested that the aircraft to the left was von Richthofen's, with Karl Emil Schäfer's aircraft in the foreground. The lower picture is believed to be von Richthofen taking off in the same Albatros, according to notes kept by Charles Donald. (*CD/PC*)

allowed, von Richthofen ascended and destroyed three enemy aircraft in January 1917. Three more followed in February, then, as the weather improved and the build-up to the Battle of Arras began, increasing air activity considerably, he downed ten more in March. This raised his score to thirty-one, with the last of them being a No. 29 Squadron Nieuport 17 fighter flown by Christopher Gilbert, who was taken prisoner and survived the war. Despite the occasional near miss, von Richthofen's star was certainly on the rise and the month ahead would see him become a national hero, helped by his deeds but also by a carefully orchestrated propaganda campaign.

By the end of March 1917 the process of turning a successful fighter pilot into a national hero was well under way. Photographs of von Richthofen had begun appearing in the press and stories of his many successes were making headlines, as shown here with issue 19 of the *Berliner Illustrirte Zeitung*. Many more would follow in the months ahead – in Germany and, more surprisingly, Britain and France. (Below) Senior officers and reporters were soon beating a path to the young ace to report on his deeds or simply bask in reflected glory. One guest was Ludwig Alexander von Falkenhausen, commander of the 6th Army, whose hair is badly in need of a military cut. Here he is captured during a visit with von Richthofen at La Brayelle towards the end of March. In April 1917, von Falkenhausen was removed from his post after the terrible losses his army sustained during the Battle of Arras. (*Author*)

# Part 4

# April to June 1917

Von Richthofen's rise to fame neatly coincided with Paul von Hindenburg's promotion, in late 1916, to Supreme Commander of the Central Powers and Chief of Staff of the German army. More importantly, some have argued, was the rise to power of his multi-talented deputy, Erich Ludendorff, who became the manipulator of all that happened in the army and on the home front, in so doing easily surpassing the influence of the Kaiser and the Reichstag, for a time. Supported by Walter Nicolai, the spymaster and the High Command's press censor, he gave propaganda an added edge in which the promotion of heroes such as von Richthofen played a central role. Very quickly a team of journalists and writers, many in uniform, descended on the young Prussian officer as his score rose and his fame spread. During April and May 1917 this interest in him reached fever pitch and his status as a German icon was assured. But they did better than they realised and created an image that spread internationally to survive this war and the one that followed.

Soon after taking office, Ludendorff expressed his concern about the state of mind and morale of Germany's civilian population, fearing that revolution might soon break out:

> The spirit of the people at home renders some action imperative. We have the best prospects of winning the war, but it is not over and what we have won must be kept. We are still a long way from that. The popular state of mind (at home and in the Army) jeopardized everything … This is now becoming a burning issue.
>
> In accordance with a proposal submitted to me by Nicolai, General Headquarters arranged for patriotic instruction to begin in the Field Army. But this is only a poor substitute for the work of enlightening public opinion at home.
>
> Nicolai, a man of unfailing industry and devotion, is responsible for the military direction of the press and the cognate duty of watching and fostering the morale of the Army and the people at home … The military censorship of the Press is another of Nicolai and his subordinates' duties … Another great branch of his work consists of the Secret Intelligence Service, prevention of spying, supervision of post, telegraph and telephone services, and the adoption of measures against industrial spying and sabotage.

It fell to Nicolai to find ways of forming these messages in an effective way using censorship to ensure such communications were handled benevolently by publishers and editors alike. Today we call this 'spinning a story' but then, as now, the end result was just the same.

The men responsible for turning von Richthofen into a national hero in an effort to encourage a war-weary population to continue fighting. Up until late 1916 Germany's efforts to milk the benefits of propaganda lagged behind the Allied powers, but all this changed when Paul von Hindenburg and his deputy, Erich Ludendorff, became Supreme Commanders of the Central Powers (top row left), shown here with their staff (third from the right and Ludendorff second from the right). (Top row right) Walter Nicolai, spymaster and propagandist par excellence, who, under Ludendorff's control, promoted, among other things, von Richthofen's life and successes. To do this various soldiers, journalists and writers were employed to meet and then write about the young Prussian officer. The main ones were (Middle row left, centre and right) George von Ompteda, Peter Lampel and George Weneger. (Bottom row left and right) Erich von Salzman, who is standing between Manfred and Lothar von Richthofen, and Kurt Tucholsky, who became editor of *Der Flieger*. (*Author*)

March and April 1917 saw official photographers visiting Jasta 11 at La Brayelle and Roucourt to take pictures of von Richthofen in action. Very quickly these photos were released and soon made headlines. Here Manfred makes ready to fly, climbs into his apparently all-red Albatros D.III and takes off on patrol, then discusses the state of play with an unidentified fellow pilot. (*CD*)

No matter how intrusive a photographer's lens became, and by April 1917 it was a daily occurrence, von Richthofen seems to have treated their presence as a necessary evil. As a result, we can view a man at the height of his powers and his war in a most candid way. Over time, despite this intrusion, he seems to have become more relaxed and occasionally even revealed a playful side to his nature. (Top left and right) Before a mission and chatting to Kurt Wolff at Roucourt and enjoying an informal moment of smiles and laughter with Wolff and Krefft. (Lower left) With Lothar von Richthofen, who joined Jasta 11 that March. (Lower right) On 15 April von Richthofen visited Jasta 12 to meet their leader and old friend, Paul Henning von Osterroht (to his right), presumably to discuss old times but also to develop fighter tactics. (*CD/Author*)

With the military determined to maintain total control of this process, it was important that professional writers, whose output could be manipulated, be employed. Very cleverly the army looked to its own ranks for such men. With millions of men in uniform, five suitable candidates who displayed these qualities were soon found – Georg von Ompteda, Erich von Salzmann, Peter Lampel, Georg Wegener and Kurt Tucholsky. In early 1917 these five noted writers had begun this task in earnest, eager to find stories that might inspire a jaded population – at home and in the trenches. So, it is of little wonder that they soon found their way to Jasta 11 and its remarkable young leader, becoming observers of his activities and those of his men.

An everyday scene for von Richthofen and Jasta 11 in April with the Battle of Arras raging beneath them, in this case Bullecourt, south-east of Arras. From the air the extent of the trenches on both sides was only too apparent, but at 4,000m and above pilots could see much more, especially the untouched land that ran quite close to front lines. On a clear day, at those heights, they might even see as far as the English Channel. (*Author*)

Of the accounts they wrote, the most interesting was commissioned by *Die Kolnische Zeitung* and written by Wegener, following a visit to La Brayelle. Having been entertained by Manfred in his quarters, Wegener briefly recalled what he saw there:

(Richthofen's) room is decorated with trophies ... the colourful national insignias and other parts taken from aircraft he has shot down. From the ceiling hangs a Gnome rotary engine modified into a chandelier ... over the door hangs the machine gun from his most dangerous opponent, the English Major Hawker.

Every pilot has his own personal aircraft, in which he always flies ... giving it a special marking that allows his comrades to keep him in sight during combat ... One machine has white, red or some other colour stripes, another carries them diagonally or vertically ... From Richthofen's eyes shine the pride of the warrior knight, whose shield and helmet ornament are known and feared by his opponents. 'I make sure my flight sees me wherever I am.'

One after the other they climb into their flying kit, which looks like a combination of a diver's suit and a Dutch fishing outfit. And with their hands in their deep pockets, laughing and joking they wander amongst the ground crew preparing their aircraft for take-off or over to a large telescope to carefully scan the sky. Even Richthofen has already put on his flying gear and carefully searches the sky with his eyes.

All of a sudden a bell hanging nearby sounds the alarm. In a moment all the mechanics run to their aircraft ... the pilots climb into their seats, the propellers thunder and one after the other they lift up and quickly climb into the blue sky. The last one to leave is Richthofen's ...

(Top) A photo believed to have been taken in the spring of 1917 showing an all-red Albatros flown by von Richthofen. The aircraft seems to have suffered damage, judging by the position of the left-hand aileron and its detached control cable, and been forced to land. (Lower) A typical scene of everyday life in Jasta 11 at Roucourt with fighters being serviced and made ready for flight. (*CD/Author*)

5 unserer erfolgreichsten Kampfflieger.

Vizefeldwebel Festner   Leutnant Schäfer
Leutnant Frhr. von Richthofen
Rittmeister Frhr. von Richthofen          Leutnant Wolff

S11
Postkartenvertrieb W. Sanke
«BERLIN N.37.»
Nachdruck wird gerichtlich verfolgt

(Above) A highly prized item in 1917 – a commemorative Sanke card showing five members of Jasta 11, two of whom have signed the card on the front and the other three, including Manfred and Lothar von Richthofen, on the back. Left to right – Sebastian Festner, Karl Allmenröder, MvR, LvR and Kurt Wolff. Of these, only Lothar would survive the war (*Author*). (Left) Charles Donald's notes that came with this negative simply states 'von Richthofen with his dog Moritz, a wounded Karl Emil Schäfer and one other in April 1917'. If so, and under the bandages it is difficult to verify Schafer's identity, the picture would have been taken before 5 June when, as commander of Jasta 28, he was killed. (*CD*)

Observers on the ground at Roucourt, viewing the scene through telescopes and binoculars, had spotted a formation of six R.E.8s from No. 59 Squadron that the German pilots soon destroyed, one of them by von Richthofen himself. To Wegener back at the airfield the combat seemed undramatic until he saw an R.E.8 crashing in flames. This quickly brought home to him the reality of aerial warfare and the level of violence it engendered. A little later he watched as the staffel returned:

> Scarcely half an hour had passed and they were all back again. The pilots climbed out of their seats and stood amongst their well-wishing comrades laughing, proud and happy while they recounted in an animated way recent events …
>
> No one was injured. It looked as though it could have been a successful sporting event. But Richthofen's machine showed how little it was like that. An enemy machine-gun burst had hit his left lower wing and the fabric looked like it had been pulled back, for about a metre and a half, by the slashing motion of a large knife. And on the outer wooden shell close to the pilot's seat ran a second tear close to the cockpit showing how another bullet had come close to ending his life.

Jasta 11's pilots pose informally on the steps of the château at Roucourt in the spring of 1917, on this occasion with Georg von Ompteda in the centre talking with some animation to von Richthofen. Von Ompteda visited Jasta 11 and then Geschwader No. 1 on a number of occasions during 1917–18 and wrote a number of strong, positive articles for the German press. (*Author*)

He influenced everybody, all of whom were obviously committed to their leader with a mixture of friendly camaraderie, great admiration and absolute obedience … As with Boelcke, Richthofen's effectiveness and value to us is not only his fighting technique, but the way he has, within his staffel, created a band of men whom he has filled with a Boelcke-type spirit, spurring them on to greater successes.

Von Salzmann was as equally impressed as Wegener when meeting von Richthofen for the first time that spring:

We were standing on a street in Douai when a small boneshaker of a car came rushing towards us. Two young officers got out and came over to me, one wore a short, undone fur coat, his hair all awry, of medium height and solid in build, and one said in a clipped, military voice, 'Richthofen'.

At the time he was just at the start of his stunning rise to fame, perhaps only one of many then. Despite this he caught my eye immediately … Richthofen possessed in abundance that inborn and appealing self-awareness and self-assurance which can never be learnt.

If there was one month in the war that has come to embody the magnitude of von Richthofen and Jasta 11's achievements it is April 1917. February and March had seen his fellow pilots begin to exercise the skills so carefully fostered by their leader and gradually hit the enemy very hard. April would see them rise to new heights, aided by a Royal Flying Corps whose aircraft were, for the moment inferior to the Albatros D.IIIs. Things would soon improve with the arrival of the S.E.5, Bristol Fighter and Sopwith Camel, but for a few months Jasta 11, in particular, 'made hay while the sun shone' and claimed 89 of the 298 aircraft believed destroyed by the German air service that month alone.

Despite their heavy losses the Royal Flying Corps did not back down. With a spring offensive due to take place on the Vimy–Arras front, followed by operations at Messines in June, Ypres a month later and Cambrai as winter approached, the stakes were too high for this to happen. With so much going on, intelligence had to be gathered by whatever means possible, no matter what the cost to the aircrew. And British commanders were only too aware of recent events when they had been caught out by the Germans' sudden withdrawal to the Hindenburg defensive line. In great secrecy, and apparently without Allied knowledge, the Germans built this immensely strong set of defences, which ran for 40 miles or more from Arras south to Soissons. Then, in a most clandestine way, aided by its fighter pilots who drove off many intruders, their ground forces withdrew to this new line in March, applying a scorched earth policy to the land they gave up to the Allies. Bearing all this in mind, the RFC were urged to redouble their efforts to ensure such an intelligence gap was not repeated. Sadly, 'Bloody April', as it became known, was the tragic result.

At the end of April 1917, Manfred's father, Albrecht, visited his sons at Roucourt and this became a much-photographed event, as shown here (top picture sitting to his son's left, lower left, middle picture on the far left, bottom picture with his sons). It is interesting to note how relaxed Manfred is in his father's presence, indicating a closeness in their relationship. On 29 April, with his father reputedly watching through a telescope from Roucourt, von Richthofen destroyed four enemy aircraft – a SPAD S.VII, an F.E.2b, a B.E.2d and a Nieuport 17, killing, or so it seems, six men in the process. In so doing he raised his list of victories to fifty-two. (*Author*)

Again a cameraman is on hand to capture von Richthofen going about his daily business. (Top left) With Leutnant Krefft in the pilot's seat, Manfred and Kurt Wolff set off on a flight, or so Charles Donald has recorded, to the Fokker works at Schwerin, presumably to view new aircraft under development there. (Top right) With Wolff possibly during this visit. (Middle picture) Date and location are not recorded by Donald but with Krefft (far left), Wolff beside him and von Richthofen present, it may have been taken on the same occasion. (Bottom left and right) Two more photos possibly at Schwerin, this time with Anthony Fokker acting as host and chauffeur. (*CD*)

This formal dinner is thought to have been in late April just before von Richthofen departed from the front on extended leave. Most guests signed copies of menus as souvenirs. Among the recognisable signatures are the von Richthofen brothers, Karl Emil Schäfer, Karl Allmenröder, Kurt Wolff and Krefft. (*Author*)

The German army's tactical withdrawal to the Hindenburg Line placed La Brayelle behind enemy lines, so forcing Jasta 11 to shift their base to Roucourt, a few miles to the south-east of Douai from where they could still easily reach the front. Here they lived comfortably in a château that adjoined the airfield, in the middle of which sat a small wood that provided some cover for the aircraft.

The battle that raged over Arras and Vimy that April was an uneven contest that just fell short of total annihilation for the Allies because of the RFC's superiority in numbers, and the aggression and resilience shown by its airmen. Even so, it was a close-run thing and cost the RFC far too many lives, with twenty-one aircraft falling to von

When flying from Roucourt
(although one source places
these two photos at Marcke
near Courtrai in June) the pilots
of Jasta 11 were accommodated
at the château adjacent to the
airfield. This location became
a regular haunt of official
photographers ever eager for
more pictures of von Richthofen
and his men for feature articles
in the press. (Top) Manfred
with Kurt Wolff probably
discussing the day's events.
(Left) On the same day joined
by Konstantin Krefft, the unit's
technical officer (second from
the left) and, it is recorded, Otto
Brauneck, who joined Jasta 11
in April and was killed in action
on 26 July 1917. (*Author*)

More visits and poses for cameras to feed an ever-growing need for news in all the magazines and newspapers appearing daily or weekly across Germany. The notes with these two negatives do not specify the date beyond being in April 1917, or the event, though both photos show the von Richthofen brothers dressed up for the occasion, which was possibly for the visit of some senior officer or VIP. (*CD*)

Richthofen alone. And as the month passed reports in the press reached a fever pitch, especially as his total of victories quickly surpassed Boelcke's and soon reached fifty-two on 29 April. Although appearing to come through all the rigours of war in fairly good condition, Manfred was no superman and when sent on leave in May he was probably in need of a rest from operational flying; and, of course, his commanders would have wanted to preserve the life of their most famous son as his propaganda value increased, if nothing else.

Before beginning his well-deserved leave Manfred was obliged to make a number of duty calls. In his memoirs he describes the weeks that followed as creating a dividing line in his life – before fame and after it had taken hold. He may have had hints of what awaited him at home, in his mailbag alone, but operational flying and leading Jasta 11 would have been too distracting for more. Now, on returning home, the full force of fame would hit him. His words capture the sense of this transition from one life to another:

> Our arrival at Cologne had been announced by telegram. People were looking out for us. On the previous day the newspapers had reported my fifty-second victory. One can only imagine what kind of a reception they had prepared for us.
>
> In the afternoon we arrived at Headquarters … First of all I met the General Commanding the Flying Services. Then, next morning the great moment when I would meet von Hindenburg and Ludendorff … It is a strange feeling to be in the rooms where the fate of the world is decided [and his fate as well]. So I was quite glad when I was outside the Holiest of Holies again to lunch with His Majesty … He congratulated me on my success and on my twenty-fifth birthday.
>
> On the following day I was to take lunch with the Kaiserin and so I flew to Hamburg. In the evening I was again invited by General Field Marshal von Hindenburg [to dinner at Bad Kreuznach] … Some days later I arrived in Schweidnitz. Although I reached there at seven o'clock in the morning, there was a large crowd waiting at the station. I was very warmly received. In the afternoon various demonstrations took place to honour me, amongst other things, by the local Boy Scouts. It became clear to me that the people at home took a vivid interest in their fighting soldiers.

Each day Kunigunde would scan these reports, taking pride in Manfred and Lothar's deeds, but growing sadder as familiar names fell on the battlefield and the war news grew ever more grave:

> We now find ourselves in a state of war with America … The enemy has lost 44 planes. Whole squadrons are said to be have been destroyed. Leutnants Voss and Berthold are mentioned. But what is this? Five of our pilots have not returned … Why is Manfred not mentioned? Prince Friedrich Karl of Prussia has died of internal bleeding … Oberleutnant Berr has fallen. Finally, Rittmeister [promoted to this rank in April having been advanced to Oberleutnant on the 23 March] von Richthofen has shot down his 38th and 39th opponents … the dice falls again …

Manfred wins his 44th aerial victory; a few days later, his total leaps to 50. He is in all the papers, on the lips of all people; flags wave over his name. Cities honour him and royalty telegraph … The enemy is totally bewildered and what they do in response is disgraceful. One day we read the headline:

Before he could begin his leave von Richthofen was obliged to undertake a number of official duties. (Top) Meeting Hindenburg on 2 May 1917, then later on, Ludendorff, who closely scrutinised his prize propaganda asset very closely, at the army's Supreme Headquarters. (Left) There was also a session with the German air services' influential leaders – General Ernst von Hoeppner (on Manfred's right) and Hermann Thomson. (Opposite) He (third from the right) then met the Kaiser, with whom he dined later as guest of honour. (*CD/Author*)

Von Richthofen was then flown by his great friend Fritz von Falkenhayn to Bad Kreuznach on 3 May to meet Kaiserin Auguste Victoria and her entourage with whom he posed for a number of photographs. (*CD/Author*)

‘English Blood Money for a German Flier! [WTB Berlin, 4 May]
The English have assembled an air squadron of volunteer fliers, said to be exclusively aimed at destroying our most successful fighter pilot, Rittmeister Freiherr von Richthofen, who has already shot down 52 enemy fliers. The pilot who succeeds in shooting down or capturing Richthofen will receive the Victoria Cross, a promotion,

The requirement to attend official events to be photographed and seen did not end with a procession of VIPs at Supreme Headquarters, but continued in Berlin with Manfred attending social gatherings, such as the Mehl-Mülhens races at Grunewald. He is talking to Prince Friedrich of Prussia, second cousin of Kaiser Wilhelm II and the elected Landrat, or district administrator, of the Frankenstein District, who also became a major general during the war. (*PC/Author*)

During May 1917 rumours were spread by the German press, undoubtedly sponsored by Walter Nicolai and his team, that an anti-Richthofen squadron had been formed deliberately to destroy the German ace. Propaganda nonsense of course, but probably based on intelligence officers reporting that the first RFC squadron (No. 56 here photographed at London Colney in April) equipped with new S.E.5 fighters had reached the front with the great British ace Albert Ball (lower picture) among their number. When von Richthofen was on leave in May, No. 56 and Jasta 11 would meet regularly head-on over the Western Front, with both sides soon realising that they had met redoubtable foes. No. 56's arrival also signalled that the domination once enjoyed by the Germans flying their Albatros DIIIs was coming to an end. (*Author*)

Once the initial rush of social events began to ease Manfred was able to slip away and find some peace while pursuing one of his favourite pursuits – hunting (top two pictures on unrecorded dates, though the left-hand picture is thought to have been taken later in 1917). But in returning home to Schweidnitz crowds again descended upon him, leaving him little time to relax as photographers continued to seek him out unrelentingly, as these pictures reveal. The lower right portrait taken with his mother, sister and youngest brother suggests that they too were fed up with the attention. A return to Jasta 11 in June may have come as something of a relief for all concerned. (*CD/Author*)

his own aeroplane as a gift, £500 sterling … A cinema cameraman will fly with the English squadron, and will record the whole incident for use in British films.'

If this report proves to be true, then the cry of a whole world, whose sons bleed in the trenches for the prestige of their countries, must answer for it.

Nevertheless, the die had been caste and the advantages and disadvantages of celebrity had to be accepted, in Manfred's case with some discomfort, as his mother recorded:

The whole city seemed mobilized. I knew how much Manfred hated to be feted. But it couldn't be helped now, he reluctantly played his part … The wonderful weather on Sunday favoured the mass hike to our house. At times, the entire street was black with people. Everyone wanted to see him. We stayed in the garden all day as delegations came and went … military bands blared … I see Manfred occupying himself with the children – how they hang onto him, how it makes him happy to look into so many young faces glowing with enthusiasm.

Only once did I see a wince cross his face – as one gentleman regretted that all two or three thousand school children could not be here to shake his hand … In the evening we could stand no more … When the onslaught did not slacken, I resorted to an extreme measure and let it be known and reported in a newspaper that he had departed. We then went away from here by car to Stanowitz, where Manfred was pleased to shoot a buck in its beautiful old hunting grounds. He longed for a few days' rest.

As we entered the town we were surprised to notice preparations for a ceremonial reception. The inhabitants lined the streets, faces looked out of all the windows, the castle flew a flag, photographs were taken and children sang songs of welcome … Manfred's face grew even more gloomy … It is becoming even harder for him to be away from the Front and his Staffel – he is pining for them.

In von Richthofen's case, his desire to return to Jasta 11 was intensified by news that his brother had been wounded on 13 May and would be sidelined until September, and that Karl Emil Schäfer had been killed in combat on 5 June 1917. His protégé, who himself had gone on to lead Jasta 28, was a great loss. So, Manfred felt compelled to attend the funeral. On the way there he also took the opportunity to pursue a campaign close to his heart and press the powers that be for new and better aircraft. Bearing in mind his own experiences with Albatros fighters, a rising number of incidents involving wing failure, especially with the new D.V model that began reaching the front in May, and an ever-strengthening enemy, this was hardly surprising. But now he could use his new-found status as a national hero to force through changes.

The Allied powers, with a combined industrial strength greater than Germany, could produce aircraft in greater numbers and this created an imbalance that might be difficult to overcome. In an effort to achieve a tactical advantage with a smaller number of fighters available, it was decided to group some Jastas together into a single mobile force. The

By the time von Richthofen became famous it had become custom and practice for portraits to be painted by noted artists of the day for public consumption  and for Sanke postcards to be produced of the nation's heroes in vast quantities. As a result, Manfred would sit for several artists that summer, including Professor Arnold Busch and Adolf Schorling, who both visited Jasta 11 and later Geschwader No. 1 to complete the two works above (examples of Busch's work to the left, Schorling's to the right). Middle) Another of the artists assigned to paint von Richthofen, Fritz Reusing (centre wearing dark jacket) with MvR and fellow pilots in the summer of 1917. (Bottom row) Just two of many Sanke cards that appeared – each one capturing a suitably heroic looking young man. (*CD/Author*)

Karl Emil Schäfer's funeral in Lille on 8 June 1917 (above and left), followed by an interment near his home in Krefeld shortly afterwards, which von Richthofen, standing in the centre of the group in the picture on the left, attended - according to notes kept by Charles Donald with this negative. However, there is a suspicion that this photograph may have been taken a few weeks later at the funeral of Karl Allmenröder, another friend and Jasta 11 stalwart, who was killed on 27 June and then buried in the Lutheran Cemetery at Wald. (*CD/Author*)

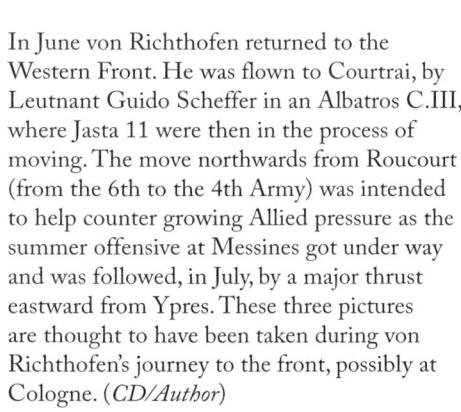

In June von Richthofen returned to the Western Front. He was flown to Courtrai, by Leutnant Guido Scheffer in an Albatros C.III, where Jasta 11 were then in the process of moving. The move northwards from Roucourt (from the 6th to the 4th Army) was intended to help counter growing Allied pressure as the summer offensive at Messines got under way and was followed, in July, by a major thrust eastward from Ypres. These three pictures are thought to have been taken during von Richthofen's journey to the front, possibly at Cologne. (*CD/Author*)

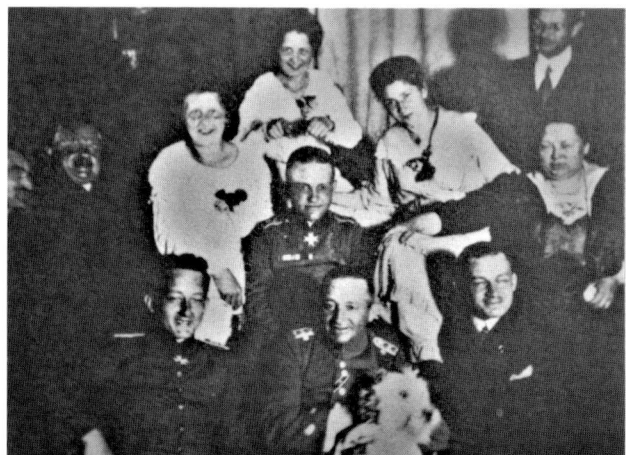

One very important feature of von Richthofen's life was his developing friendship with Werner Voss, with whom he served in Jasta 2 in late 1916, and the Voss family, who hailed from Krefeld. In many ways it was an attraction of opposites. Werner had, by all accounts, an outward-going, almost unconventional personality, while Manfred was more formal and reserved in his habits, although he did display a sense of fun at times. And yet the relationship worked and this led to at least two visits to Krefeld during 1917, captured here in great detail by official and unofficial photographers. Some of these pictures were published in the press and others appeared as a group of Sanke cards. Von Richthofen flew to Krefeld in a two-seater, while Voss arrived in his heavily personalised Albatros D.III, with both men being met by members of the Voss family and some casual observers. Voss joined JG I, in command of Jasta 10, during that July, and was killed the following September in action. Von Richthofen was, it has been reported, deeply affected by his friend's death and remained in contact with Voss senior. It seems as though Manfred was due to visit the Voss family in April 1918 when he too was killed. (*CD/Author*)

first of these to be formed would operate under the 4th Army's banner and not the 6th Army's, which Jasta 11 had served up to that time. In theory, this large formation could move, at a moment's notice, to any part of the front where the enemy were particularly active and achieve temporary superiority. At the same time, German reconnaissance aircraft would operate behind enemy lines, mostly without escorts, using their ability to climb high over the battlefield to avoid the RFC's fighters. As needs must, of course, but with such a large group of fighters sweeping the front it stood a chance of success. However, this depended heavily on the quality of Germans' aircraft, the pilots and the skill with which they were led.

It was these changes and more that von Richthofen, and the other Jastaführers, would most certainly have been briefed on during May and June. This may even have hastened his return to the front. Such a strong, clear-headed leader would wish to be there to make sure that his ideas were implemented in such a way as to make the new, enlarged formation a success. In this though, he faced a major stumbling block, in the form of Hauptmann Otto Bufe, *Kommandeur der Flieger* (Kofl) of the 4th Army, under whom von Richthofen would soon serve.

As part of this reorganisation, and to meet expected British attacks at Messines and Ypres that Summer, Jasta 11 had moved to Bavikhove a few kilometres north-east of Courtrai. It was here that Jasta 11 would be grouped together with Jastas 6, 7 and 26, operating under the command of Bufe. But before this took effect the Jastas involved changed, with 11 being joined by 4, 6 and 10 instead.

Very soon, though, cracks began to appear in this plan and a clash of wills between von Richthofen and Bufe followed. In a case of an experienced fighter pilot and national hero, just beginning to realise the power he possessed in determining the future course of aviation in war, and an equally well established officer, but with far less experience in these matters, there was only ever likely to be one winner.

The main point of difference between von Richthofen and Bufe seems to have been over the way the new formation should operate and the Kofl's desire to maintain strict control over all they did. To do this Bufe wanted to stick to a timetable of standing patrols over the front undertaken by small groups of fighters in what were called *Sperrflüge* operations. These simply involved flying up and down the lines on a set course creating the illusion of a defensive shield to deter enemy patrols. Von Richthofen felt that this was wrong, believing that the tactics introduced by Boelcke still held good and should be applied to these new, larger groups. It was a dispute that became even more pronounced when Manfred was appointed commander of the first Jagdgeschwader on 25 June.

As a Jastaführer his views would have carried some weight, but as leader of JG I his authority grew even greater. This was also helped by the fact that the order appointing him, signed by Thomsen, contained the words, 'The Geschwader is a closed unit. It is appointed for the purpose of fighting for and securing aerial superiority in crucial combat sectors.' To this von Hoeppner added the words, 'The Geschwader is a self-contained unit. Its duty is to achieve and maintain air superiority in sectors of the Front as directed,' later injecting, 'In the person of Rittmeister von Richthofen it has a

(Left) A photo taken in September or October 1916 shortly after von Richthofen joined Oswald Boelke's Jasta 2, which formed at Bertincourt in August that year. (Right) According to Charles Donald, this picture of von Richthofen was possibly taken in 1917 when paying a visit to Fokker's Schwerin Works. I have no reason to doubt this. (*CD/Author*)

Von Richthofen's success flying with Jasta 2 resulted in the award of the Pour le Mérite during January 1917, and the presentation of this glass, silver and gold goblet. In painting his aircraft all red, or some partially so, he made an indelible impression on the minds of friend and foe alike. The photo above was taken in spring 1917 and shows von Richthofen's Albatros D.III, second in line, at Douai after he had assumed command of Jasta 11. (*CD/Author*)

As von Richthofen's fame spread, during the spring of 1917, so journalists and photographers found their way to Jasta 11 to meet and report on the growing accomplishments of this young man. On this occasion von Richthofen sat in his red Albatros at Roucourt with his pilots gathered around him. In due course many of these men would also be trumpeted as 'heroes of the air' but none would achieve the same status as *Der Rote Kampfflieger*, as he would soon become known. (*CD/Author*)

Von Richthofen's rapidly growing fame soon resulted in a flood of headlines (left) and posed photographs (middle) that were released to the press and sold in huge quantities as postcards. There were also a number of formal portraits – as here painted by the well-known artist Rudolf Bauer, which appeared on the cover of the art magazine *Jugend* in 1917. (*Author*)

More paintings followed (left), in this case by Fritz Reusing, which went on display in early 1918. This portrait was presented to Manfred's parents and was lost when the Russians overran the family home towards the end of the Second World War. (Middle) Von Richthofen's lucky charm, now on display at the RAF Museum in London. (Right) A treasured gift sent by Ilse von Richthofen to 'my dear brother Manfred'. (*Author*)

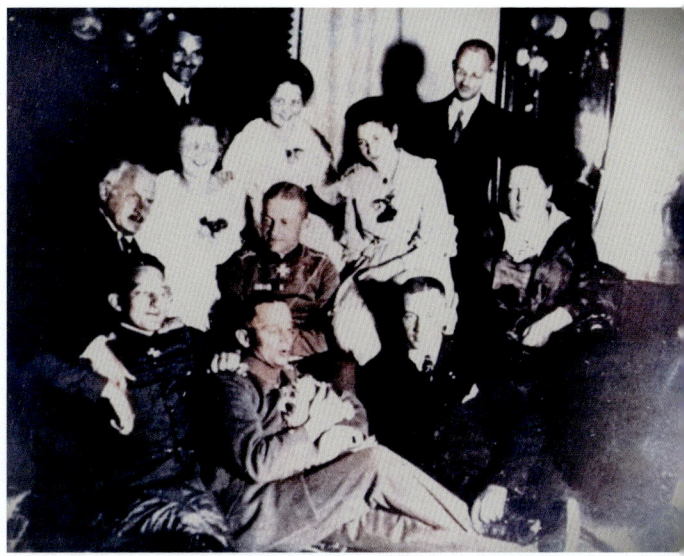

Front-line duties absorbed most of von Richthofen's time and energy, but this was occasionally interspersed by duty visits elsewhere. (Above left) At Schwerin again with (L to R) Lt Konstantin Krefft, Manfred's Technical Officer in Jasta 11 and, later, Geschwader No. 1, Anthony Fokker and Kurt Wolff, a fellow ace from Jasta 11 and a close friend, who would die in combat during September. (Above right) Manfred and Werner Voss became good friends and in 1917 von Richthofen visited the Voss home in Krefeld – events that were much photographed, with some becoming Sanke cards in the process. (Below left) More portraits continued to appear, including this one by Rudolf Bauer. (Below right) A posed but wonderfully cheerful picture of Manfred and fellow JG I pilots. (*CD/Author*)

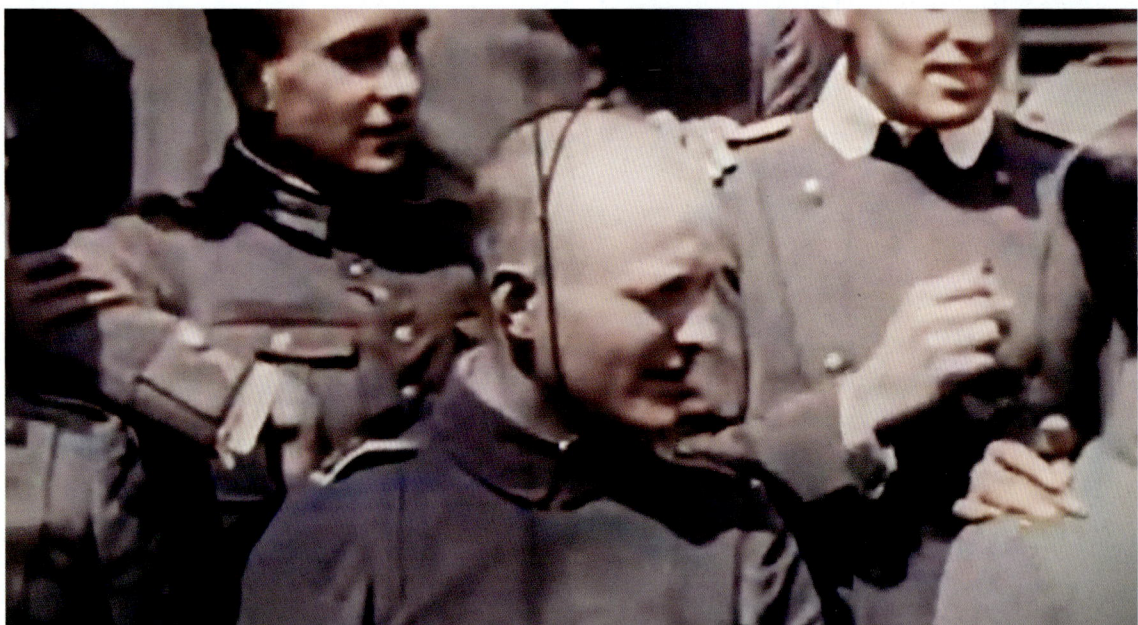

A severe head wound on 6 July 1917 shook the once supremely self-assured von Richthofen and profoundly affected his personality. The two pictures above (left and right), taken only two or so months apart, seem to convey the changes that took place and the self-doubt that entered his mind. It seems that the wound still required frequent treatment up to his death in April 1918. The mental scars would probably have taken longer, recovery exacerbated by combat fatigue. (Below) Even though badly wounded, he still turned out to be filmed, as shown here, when required to satisfy ever-pressing propaganda needs. His drawn looks are only too apparent, as is the dressing strapped in place to protect his still open wound. (*Author*)

(Above left) Von Richthofen's dog Moritz remained a constant companion and caring for the Great Dane gave him with a much-needed distraction from the demands of leading men in battle and being a much-publicised national hero. The dog, in turn, appeared in many photographs and cine films churned out for public consumption. Moritz survived his master's death and apparently returned to Germany with Alfred Gerstenberg, with whom he lived into old age. (Right) Another gift from or to von Richthofen, given or received in 1917, this time a silver box containing cigars and cigarettes, to which he was partial. The box is inscribed with his signature and the words 'Marckebeeke 2nd August 1917'. It is recorded that a number of enemy aircrew who survived encounters with him, received gifts of cigars, at least twice from him personally. (*CD/Author*)

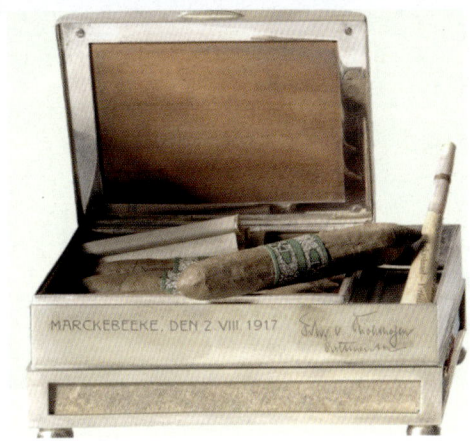

In late summer 1917 the Fokker Dr.1 Triplane began to arrive on the Western Front, hopefully offering fighter pilots a combat aircraft better than the Albatros D.V or Pfalz D.III, which tended to be outclassed by new enemy aircraft such as the Sopwith Camel and S.E.5. (Above left) What is thought to be the prototype Dr.1 in flight at Schwerin. (Above right) Anthony Fokker, in the cockpit, demonstrating the first production triplane, No. 102/17, to Major General Fritz von Lossberg, Chief of staff of the 4th Army, and von Richthofen. Other VIPs included Ludendorff and Georg Michaelis, German Chancellor between July and October 1917. (*CD/Author*)

Once Ludendorff had risen to power he set in motion a very active propaganda programme, managed by Walter Nicolai, that included the exploitation of von Richthofen's name and reputation. There was extensive press coverage of all he did and his exploits were even trumpeted in bright yellow posters that were each day placed on notice boards around the country, such as the one shown here on which his seventy-first, seventy-second and seventy-third victories were announced. (*Author*)

**Militärischer Tagesbericht der Münchner Neuesten Nachrichten**

München. Donnerstag, 28. März 1918. nachmittags 1½ Uhr

Amtliche Meldung. W.T.B. Großes Hauptquartier, 28. März vormittags

**Westlicher Kriegsschauplatz**

Auf dem Schlachtfeld in Frankreich führte der Engländer erneut frische, aus anderen Fronten herausgezogene Divisionen unseren Truppen entgegen.

Nordwestlich von Bapaume warfen wir den Feind aus alten Trichterstellungen auf Bucquoy und Hébuterne. Mit besonderer Zähigkeit kämpfte der Feind vergeblich um die Wiedereroberung von Albert. Starke, von Panzerwagen begleitete Angriffe brachen auf den Hängen der der Stadt westlich vorgelagerten Höhen blutig zusammen.

Südlich von der Somme bahnten sich unsere Divisionen an vielen Stellen den Weg durch alte feindliche Stellungen und warfen Engländer und Franzosen in das seit 1914 vom Kriege unberührt gebliebene Gebiet von Frankreich zurück.

**Die siegreichen Truppen des Deutschen Kronprinzen haben in unaufhaltsamem Angriff von St. Quentin über die Somme die feindlichen Stellungen in 60 km Tiefe eingestoßen.**

Sie drangen gestern bis Pierrepont vor und haben Montdidier genommen.

Unsere Verluste halten sich in normalen Grenzen, an einzelnen Brennpunkten sind sie schwerer. Die Zahl der Leichtverwundeten wird auf 60 bis 70 vom Hundert aller Verluste geschätzt.

An der lothringischen Front nahmen die Artilleriekämpfe an Stärke zu.

Rittmeister Frhr. v. Richthofen errang seinen 71., 72. und 73. Luftsieg.

Von den anderen Kriegsschauplätzen nichts Neues.

Der Erste Generalquartiermeister Ludendorff.

After some teething problems with the Fokker Dr.1, involving wing failures, the type was withdrawn while modifications took place. During this time von Richthofen reverted to the Albatros D.V. By early 1918 the Dr.1s were back with this example, thought to be either No. 477/17 or No. 425/17, both it seems painted red overall, and flown by Manfred. If 425/17 it is the aircraft in which he met his death on 21 April 1918. (*CD/Author*)

There has been some debate whether this photo was taken of von Richthofen (in the centre of the group) and his men at Cappy on 21 April 1918 or a few days earlier at Lechelle. Lt Richard Wenzl, to whom the picture is often credited, confirmed the 21st, but a doubt still exists. Either way, it shows how Manfred, and some of the men he flew with on the 21st, would have appeared on that singular day in his short life. (*CD/Author*)

Von Richthofen's death on 21 April was celebrated on the British side of the lines and his Triplane was quickly stripped of anything moveable, as the photos above bear witness. Remarkably, considering he was responsible for the deaths of so many Allied airmen, he was honoured with a full military funeral the next day, although later on his grave was reputably desecrated by less-forgiving local citizens. (*CD/Author*)

Many items relating to von Richthofen, mostly souvenired from his crashed triplane, survive in public and private hands as this selection makes clear, some having been turned into practical, everyday use objects. (*CD/Author*)

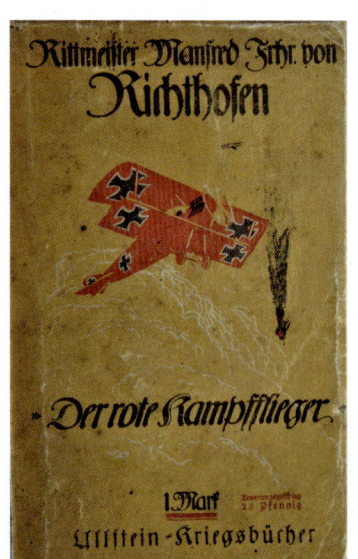
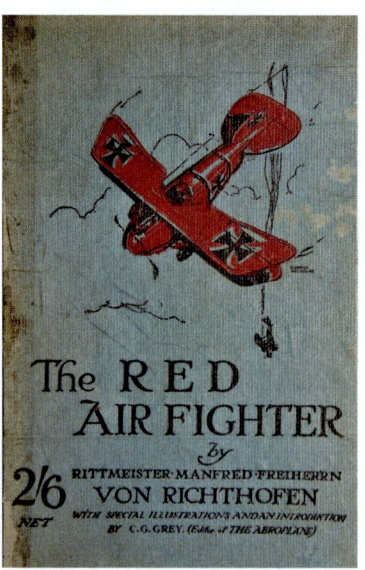

Due to the work of some expert propagandists von Richthofen's name became very well-known at home but also in the enemy camp. This was helped considerably by the publication of his memoirs during the war in Germany and Britain – as the two pictures above confirm. But, perhaps more potently, were the glamourous, but somewhat brooding images of a young hero that were produced in vast quantities during the war. (Above right) This is perhaps the best example of this image making work. (*CD/Author*)

(Where photos have been colourised this work was undertaken by my old friend David Knowles or myself).

commander whose steel-hard will in relentlessly pursuing the enemy will infuse every member of the Geschwader.'

With this backing von Richthofen was given carte blanche to operate as he thought fit and it probably helped that Crown Prince Rupprecht of Bavaria, who commanded the 2nd, 4th and 6th armies at the time, added his own support in a carefully worded telegram dated the 24th June. In it he reiterated the point that JG I was a 'closed unit', with its purpose being 'to win and secure dominance in the air'. All this would have given von Richthofen added muscle if he wished to challenge anything Bufe might care to institute. However, it wasn't the end of the matter and the differences between the two men would continue to fester. They resurfaced during July 1917 when the Rittmeister was on an enforced absence from the front.

# Part 5

# July to December 1917

If a reminder were needed that flying was a deadly business, then two deaths in June 1917 gave von Richthofen just such a prompt. Since January he had bonded very closely with the pilots of Jasta 11, with whom he had shared great success and some losses. Among them was, of course, his brother, but then there were others such as Kurt Wolff, Karl Allmenröder and Karl Emil Schäfer. Sadly, in June, the last two of these fell to the enemy, each death reminding Manfred of his own mortality. It was a state of mind that would not have been helped by two other deaths in battle at this time – those of his, cousin Oskar von Schickfuss, and his old and trusted friend, Georg Zeumer.

So, by July, when settling into his command of Jagdgeschwader No. 1, the sense of invincibility Manfred seems to have possessed was probably slowly being eaten away.

War is an attritional business, and no one is immune from its effects, though some can go on longer than others, through force of will or if possessing great inner strength or simply by luck. But there will always be a limit and the many pressures Manfred was facing that summer were of a most taxing nature. There were the dangers of combat, the stresses imposed by flying in an open cockpit in pitiless conditions without protection from the elements, G forces, noxious materials and more. There was also the emotional strain of losing friends to consider, plus a growing awareness that his country was

A view of the battlefield that was only too familiar to von Richthofen and his men in June and July 1917. This photograph was taken from a German observation balloon showing British gunfire and clouds of poison enveloping their front line. (*Author*)

By June 1917 von Richthofen was much older and wiser than the eager young pilot recruited by Oswald Boelcke less than a year earlier, as these three photos reveal. Already an accomplished and widely celebrated ace, he now took on the responsibility of heading a large new fighter group, JG I, in an increasingly bitter war. It was a role that would test his resolve and his leadership qualities to the full. (*Author*)

probably fighting a losing battle. And he could see for himself that shortages of food and raw material were draining a once buoyant Germany and slowly stripping its people of a will to fight. Then there were the draining effects of being an exploited national hero to contend with and by July his status could not have been higher or the level of intrusion into his private life greater. Being at the front, despite the close proximity of death each day, was probably the lesser of two evils.

Having taken command of JG I and moved to the 4th Army front, the last days of June and early July would have found von Richthofen tied up by a myriad number of organisational and domestic duties. He still found time to fly and would have set about the business, as Boelcke had done, of briefing and training his men in the tactics he wished to employ. Hauptmann Bufe was for the moment held in check by the directives von Richthofen had received but was not a spent force and only awaited an opportunity to reassert his authority. This arrived on 6 July.

While JG I was being formed, von Richthofen took whatever opportunities he could to fly again and probably quickly discovered that the pace of the war had changed with new and better types of enemy aircraft beginning to equip many RFC squadrons. The

(Left) Lothar von Richthofen's presence in Jasta 11 must have been reassuring to his brother, but during May he was recovering from a serious injury and would not return until July. Manfred probably felt his absence keenly, but an old friend (Right), Alfred Gerstenberg, was on hand to provide the comradeship he undoubtedly needed. (Opposite) The Albatros D.V began to arrive that summer, but it did not give the hoped for improvement in performance von Richthofen demanded, and it came, like the D.III, with structural weaknesses. These two pictures capture D.V No. 1177/17, partially painted in red, that he flew that summer and in which he was severely wounded on 6 July. (*CD/Author*)

speed of his victories in April had been staggeringly high but was now unlikely to be repeated, especially with the Albatros D.IIIs, now supplemented by the D.Vs, the best the Germans could offer. However, the draw of combat must have been very strong and further successes soon followed. On 18 June von Richthofen destroyed an R.E.8 and killed its crew, Ralph Ellis, from Surbiton in Surrey, and Harold Barlow, who hailed from Cheshire. Then five days later he sent down a SPAD S.VII while flying Albatros D.V No. 1177/17, partially painted red, a DH.4 on 24 June and a second DH.4 in the same fighter on the day his appointment to command JG I was confirmed. And July began with one more success. On 2 July he incinerated the crew of an R.E.8 from No. 53 Squadron near Deûlémont, according to his combat report.

With the Allied thrust towards Arras fading into memory and the expected main British campaign of the year before Ypres due to begin in July, the RFC were fully

involved in trying to control the skies over the battlefield and gather information about enemy dispositions. Despite its fledgling status, JG I rose each day to meet an increasingly aggressive enemy when the weather allowed; and that summer heavy rain flooded this notoriously waterlogged land, making it almost impassable even without the effects of continuous artillery fire. On 6 July, in an effort to stem this flow, von Richthofen took off with some of his men from Markebeeke in what should have been just another patrol, but on this occasion nearly ended in disaster, as Manfred later reported:

Four views of von Richthofen's Albatros D.V No. 1177/17 (above and facing page) after he had force-landed having been hit on top of his head by a bullet thought to have been fired by the observer flying in a No. 20 Squadron F.E.2b, or it may also have been a case of friendly fire, such was the nature of aerial warfare at that time. (*CD/Author*)

We had flown for quite a while between Ypres and Armentieres without contacting the enemy. Then I saw a formation on the other side … We had a favourable wind from the east and I watched them fly some distance behind lines. I cut off their retreat … My opponent turned and accepted battle … he flew towards me, and I hoped to get on his tail and open fire. Suddenly, something struck my head. For a moment my whole body was immobilised. My arms hung down limply by my side; my legs flopped loosely beyond my control. Worst of all, a nerve leading to my eyes had been paralysed and I was completely blind.

I felt my aircraft plummeting downwards … Suddenly, it occurred to me that this was what it felt like to be shot down and die. Any moment I expected my wings to break off [as he had seen so often before when others went down]. I didn't lose my wits for a moment and soon recovered control over my arms and legs and could grip the controls again. Mechanically, I cut off the engine, but what good does it do? I can't fly without my sight. I forced my eyes open – tore off my goggles – but even then I couldn't see the sun. I was completely blind. The seconds seemed to pass in an eternity.

Occasionally, my aircraft caught itself, only to slip away again. At the beginning I was at a height of 3,500 metres and now I must have fallen at least 1,800 or 2,700 metres. I focussed all my energy and said to myself, 'I must see – I must – I must see!' Whether this helped I do not know, but suddenly I could see black and white spots and slowly regained my eyesight. I looked at the sun – could stare straight into it without feeling the least pain. It seemed as though I were looking through thick black glass.

Again I controlled the machine and continued gliding down. Nothing but shell holes beneath me. A big forest came into sight and I realised that I was inside our lines … I wanted to land immediately, for I didn't know how long I might remain conscious. I noticed that my strength was leaving me and everything was turning black again … I landed my aircraft without any great difficulty, tearing down some telephone wires … I tumbled out of the machine and could not rise again.

I had a good-sized hole in my head – a wound of about ten centimetres in length – the bare white skull bone lay exposed [and he was running a slightly raised temperature, which in the circumstance is not unusual].

Meanwhile, the whole episode was witnessed on the ground by trained observers watching activity over the front through a high-powered telescope. An air defence officer, Leutnant Hans Schröder, recalled in his book *An Airman Remembers*:

Then Richthofen's red aircraft suddenly turned on its nose and dived down out of the throng of combatants … I kept my eye focussed on him. Nothing seemed to impede his downward rush – he was finished … Then – two hundred metres above the ground – he caught the machine and flew straight towards me … it landed and taxied. I looked through my Zeiss glasses and saw Richthofen climb out, stagger and fall … I reached him as he lay with his head resting on his leather helmet, while a stream of blood trickled down from the back of his head. His eyes were closed and his face was as white as a sheet.

'Are you in pain?' I asked. 'I feel better now. I want to go to (the hospital) Courtrai at once.' … Then the ambulance arrived and we laid him carefully on the stretcher and put him inside. I got in beside him … I stayed with him while the doctors examined his wound [at Field Hospital No. 76] … he was put under anaesthetic, the hair around the injury was shaved and the surgeon [Professor Doctor Paul Kraske, who was a cancer specialist] probed the wound carefully. Luckily it was not of a dangerous sort … I went back to my post.

Later on that day, having examined the wound, Dr Kraske wrote an interim report, which in the event undoubtedly made too little of its severity:

> The perforation is to the bone. The bone shows only superficial roughness. There is no other injury … The entire wound was excised within healthy tissue [all dead tissue, bone debris and foreign bodies, material from his flying helmet, for example, being removed, leaving only healthy tissue when suturing began]. Fairly strong bleeding. Several catgut sutures through the galea [fibrous tissue that covers the upper part of the skull], skin sutures with silk.

As his treatment progressed Kraske would re-evaluate his findings and present a more detailed picture:

> Without a doubt there has been a severe concussion of the brain and even probably a haemorrhage. For this reason, sudden changes in air pressure during flight might lead to disturbances of consciousness … he must not resume flying before being given permission to do so by a physician.

With advances in medicine head injuries of this seriousness have become subject to a complex range of treatments. Being hit so violently by a bullet travelling at high velocity can have many damaging outcomes, but in 1917 this was barely recognised.

Today a wound of this sort is described as a traumatic brain injury (TBI) and is known to have many long-lasting effects. Even at the lower end of the scale, these can manifest themselves in physical, cognitive, social, emotional and behavioural ways. For example, some of the key effects noted by doctors over the years include headaches, dizziness, reduced spatial awareness, diminished powers of recall and concentration impairment, depression and often paranoia, anxiety, seizures, difficulty sleeping, problems with eyesight, reduced motor skills and more. And these can last for months, if not years, depending upon the nature of a person's way of life – physical and mental stresses, age, general health and so on.

So how severe was von Richthofen's wound and what problems may it have caused him in the months that followed? The first thing to note is the effect of a bullet moving at great speed hitting the bilateral parietal bone in his skull, especially as its path of travel caused damage to the bone's central fibrous joint, the sagittal suture and the adjoining lambdoid and coronal sutures.

Although the impact in this case created a non-penetrating lesion, it still seems to have fractured the skull. Such was the force of the blow that it cleaved the skin open and splintered the exposed parietal bone. The shockwave set off would have been an extreme one, violently shaking the brain and doing untold damage in the process, including,

St Nicholas' Hospital Courtrai (during the war designated Field Hospital No. 76) as it appeared in 1917 when von Richthofen became a patient there. (*CD*)

When admitted to Field Hospital No. 76 Manfred came under the immediate care of the noted pre-war cancer specialist, now in uniform, Professor Paul Kraske (above left) and Nurse Katie Otersdorf, who would feature in a number of official photographs, taken, one presumes, for propaganda purposes. (*Author/CD*)

in von Richthofen's case, temporary blindness. This, in medical terms, was caused by a compression of the vertebral artery within the transverse foramen of the neck. The vertebral artery gets stressed and then compressed, thereby shutting down blood flow from the vertebral artery into the brain. This in turn shuts down the blood supply to the occipital lobe, which processes visual information in the brain. This lack of blood flow results in temporary blindness.

By tremendous good fortune von Richthofen survived, but the consequences of his injury were far from clear and the hard-pressed doctors who tended him would have had a limited range of therapies to explore beyond the surgical repair of an open wound. Whatever else happened, he was left to his own devices and could expect no help in treating the other effects of his injury. Being a self-possessed man of great inner strength, he undoubtedly tried to push these things to one side, but psychological wounds cannot be easily cured by willpower alone and the consequences of that day in July were unlikely to leave him for a long time. Being a commander and a front-line fighter pilot, daily courting death, was probably the worst environment in which to recover and could, perhaps, even make the symptoms worse.

Anthony Fokker, who knew von Richthofen quite well by then, probably best summed up the changes the injury wrought in the young ace. He recorded that:

The news of his fall was kept from the German public, which superstitiously regarded him as a superman, beyond death. It was less than a month before he was back in the air again, but never as his old self. Something had gone out of him … Now he knew that death could reach out for him as the others, and this is no knowledge for an airman to live with, day and night.

Inevitably, when the story reached the press, the public's reaction was indeed a profound one, resulting in a flood of mail to JG I in the field and von Richthofen's home at Schweidnitz. However, by the time this happened von Richthofen, rightly or wrongly, had returned to operational duty, probably against the advice of medical staff, but motivated by a keen sense of duty. In any case, he could read for himself reports of what was happening at the front, as the Allies continued to push forward, and understood how hard-pressed his comrades were, with Oberleutnant Kurt-Bertram von Döring acting as commander in his absence. In the circumstances it is unlikely that he would stay away for long at such a critical time, despite the state of his health.

His early return may also have been encouraged by the heavy casualties the unit was sustaining, plus Hauptmann Bufe's renewed interference in JG I's operations. Where von Richthofen promoted a high degree of flexibility in deterring enemy action, the 4th Army's Kofl continued to advocate a far more rigid flying programme concentrating the four Jastas of JG I in the air at the same time at different heights, so creating a the illusion of an air 'barricade'. So, a difference of opinion that had first arisen in June quickly re-emerged and caused von Richthofen to flex his political muscle, with unhappy consequences for Bufe. All these debates merged quickly into a letter written

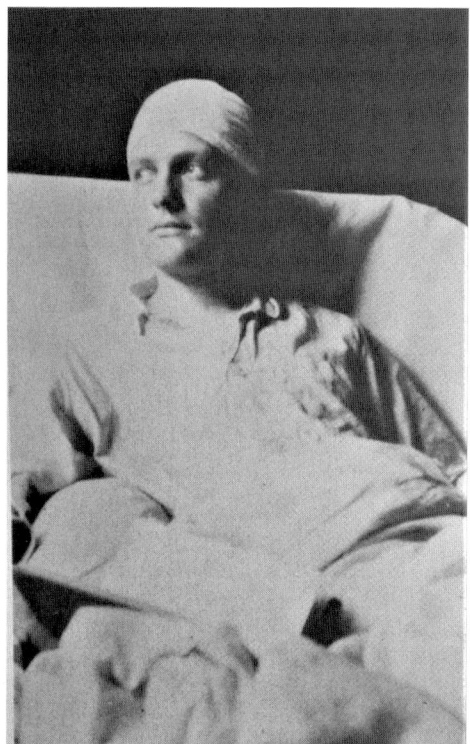

It appears that news of von Richthofen's wounding on 6 July was deliberately kept from the press, Nicolai and his associates presumably concerned about its damaging effect on morale at home. True or not, any news of von Richthofen's war exploits was limited until September 1917. However, this did not stop official photographers visiting Field Hospital No. 76 to disturb Manfred's recovery, as demonstrated here with Katie Otersdorf, his father, the artist Arnold Busch and some of his pilots, including Kurt Wolff, who was also hospitalised with an arm wound. For medical staff used to treating head injuries the distant, almost haunted look on his face is only too familiar. By the time he was visited by this fellow officer, possibly his temporary successor with JG I, Oberleutnant Kurt-Bertram von Döring, or Rittmeister Karl Heino Grieffenhagen, leader of Jasta 18, (bottom right), he seems to have regained some semblance of normality, albeit undoubtedly strained. (*CD/Author*)

by von Richthofen on the 18th to old friend and fellow pilot Fritz von Falkenhayn, who was by then Ernst von Hoeppner's personal staff officer at headquarters. In this role von Falkenhayn wielded some influence, especially being the only son of Erich von Falkenhayn, Chief of the General Staff until August 1916, and still a man of tremendous power in Germany. Von Richthofen must have been aware of this and probably chose to exploit Falkenhayn's position to get his own way in this localised argument between two officers of comparatively junior rank.

The wording of von Richthofen's letter was provocative to say the least and possibly incautious. Passages of complaint, such as these below, litter his communication:

> When an enemy aircraft has been shot down recently, it was done only by the Jagdgeschwader. What are the other 12 Staffelns doing [there being sixteen on 4th Army's front]? This is not due to individual pilots or Staffel leaders but lies elsewhere. When I came to this Army Bufe said to me, 'It does not matter to me that enemy aircraft are shot down … rather that your Jagdstaffel by its presence at the front will barricade the air!' This is an insanely great mistake, one could not make a bigger one …
>
> The other Jagdstaffeln are unhappy about it. The Jagdgeschwader is a thorn in his side … So now he uses the opportunity of my being sick to issue idiotic orders to do with the way the Geschwader should operate, how take-off preparations should go etc, as if he was the Commander of the Geschwader.
>
> I can assure you that it is no fun these days to be the leader of a Jagdstaffel in this Army. In the 6th Army, after all, I had the good Sorg, who had no grasp at all of fighter tactics and the purpose of a Jagdstaffel. This Bufe is prejudiced in such a way that it is impossible to deal with him … For the past three days the British have done what they want. They come over, fly wherever they want and completely dominate the air … Almost none at all are shot down [not entirely true, because in the period from the 7th to the 18th July, when Manfred wrote this letter, JG I claimed approximately thirty-three aircraft and balloons destroyed, against three dead, three wounded and one a prisoner of war].
>
> Our aircraft are, quite frankly, shockingly inferior to the British. The Sopwith Triplane and 200hp SPAD, as well as the Sopwith Camel single-seater play with our D.Vs. In addition to having better-quality aircraft they have many more … The people at home have not brought out any new machines for almost a year, only these lousy D.Vs, and have remained stuck with the Albatros D.IIIs in which I fought in the autumn of last year.

Although returning to JG I on 25 July, Manfred, it seems, was forbidden to fly by medical officers and had to visit the hospital at Courtrai for further treatment to have more bone splinters removed. While this happened the wound would have had to be reopened, so prolonging recovery. Nevertheless, he decided, on his own volition to fly again, but this quickly reminded him that all was not well.

Despite the severity of von Richthofen's wound he still carried out many of his duties and wherever he went cameras seem to have followed – some official, others purely opportunistic. (Top left) With Katie Otersdorf for public consumption. (Top right) Attending an event to celebrate the award of the Pour le Mérite to Oberleutnant Eduard Dostler of Jasta 6. On this occasion it seems that von Richthofen placed his own decoration around Dostler's neck, the Oberleutnant's having yet to arrive. (Middle) Attending a dinner, still with a heavily bandaged head, with some members of JG I at Château Bethune near Markebeeke. (Bottom) Captured by the camera as he leaves an unrecorded event. (*CD*)

(Top) Von Richthofen poses with mostly enlisted members of Jasta 11 to celebrate the unit's 200th victory by Hans-Georg von der Osten on the 17th. (Middle) Attending Ludendorff's visit to Markebeeke on 19 August, a duty undertaken so that the general could presumably inspect his prize propaganda asset. (Lower left and right) News of von Richthofen's injury was kept from the public for sometime. During this time the press coninued to produce pictures such a these to remind a ever eager readership that their hero still existed. (*CD/Author*)

After having suffered such a severe wound it was important for propaganda purposes that he appear in public so that any concerns about his state of health be quickly nullified. An opportunity for this came on 21st August with a parade at Courtrai for the Kaiser. It is quite likely that von Richthofen's presence was essential to the success of this event. Nearly all the photographs that have survived have Manfred centre stage – as the pictures above and on the adjoining page bear witness. He certainly received more attention that the Kaiser, who by late 1917 was becoming an increasingly unpopular figure (*CD/Author*)

(Lower left and right) These two 'unofficial' photos of the event only recently came to light. The first shows Manfred as centre of attention being greeted warmly by the Kaiser with an official photographer close by to capture the moment. The second taken a little later when the Kaiser has moved on with his entourage leaving Manfred to make his way back to JG1 and a difficult future. (*Author*)

As the summer passed and his wound slowly healed, von Richthofen began flying again, despite feeling nauseous and dizzy when he did so. Photographers captured his return to duty and their work gives us a glimpse of his life then – his head wound now covered with a smaller dressing held in place by a strap secured under his chin. He seems to have joined in the banter so necessary to young men, especially when facing combat each day. (Lower right) Charles Donald recorded that this picture was taken 'when a party of nurses, including Katie Otersdorf, visited von Richthofen in late August, early September'. (*CD/Author*)

On the 16th, during a patrol with four of his men, von Richthofen claimed to have shot down a Nieuport 17 for his fifty-eighth victory. On feeling the effects of G force, noise, fumes and raised blood pressure, as his Albatros gained height, he experienced dizziness and felt himself to be in danger of collapse. Nevertheless, he carried on stalking the enemy fighter, sending it down near the Houthulst Forest, north-east of Ypres. As he did so, a severe reaction set in, and he felt so sick and dizzy that he quickly returned to base to recover. However, in his combat report he recorded that this was due to coming down to 'about 50 metres behind him [the enemy aircraft]', where, 'I flew through a cloud of gas from the explosion so that, for a brief moment, I became ill.' In deflecting the cause of his early return from his head wound to the effects of battlefield gas, he obviously hoped to deceive his commanders into believing he was fit to fly again, when clearly he wasn't.

He was only partially successful in this because on the 18th a telegram arrived from von Hoeppner congratulating von Richthofen on his success, but adding:

> I expect he is cognizant of the responsibility of deploying his person, and that he will fly only if absolute necessity warrants it until he has overcome the last traces of his wound.

There could not have been a clearer admonishment of von Richthofen's behaviour, and this was not Bufe but a man of real authority who was unlikely to treat disobedience lightly, no matter how famous the transgressor. The general, who seems to have been a compassionate man, would have taken this line as a matter of course, but he would also have been aware of Manfred's importance in helping boost the morale of people at home. He, and the High Command, could ill afford to lose such a potent symbol of national prestige. It was a difficult balance to achieve. Without further victories his newsworthiness might diminish, but death could be even more damaging. And then there was the man himself, with his gradually evaporating reserves of energy, to consider.

Nevertheless, von Richthofen did fly again and on 26 August shot down a SPAD S.VII from 19 Squadron, seeing it explode near the ground, and killing its pilot, Coningsby Williams, a young man from Leicester. During the action, 'due to poor incendiary ammunition' his Albatros sustained damage to its pressure line, intake manifold and exhaust. As a result, the engine appears to have failed, forcing von Richthofen to glide eastwards towards his airfield, which presumably he reached without having to force land. Interestingly, his combat report seems to have elicited a stern reminder from 4th Army that the order of 12 August, which grounded von Richthofen unless it was absolutely essential that he fly, be obeyed. The reminder also said 4th Army 'asks to be notified in case this point is not satisfactorily taken into account'.

A desire to lead from the front, and help secure his position at the same time, undoubtedly encouraged Manfred to ignore any instructions he had been given that effectively grounded him and fly again. In this case he may also have been encouraged to do so by the arrival of the first two Fokker Dr.I Triplanes at the front, accompanied by

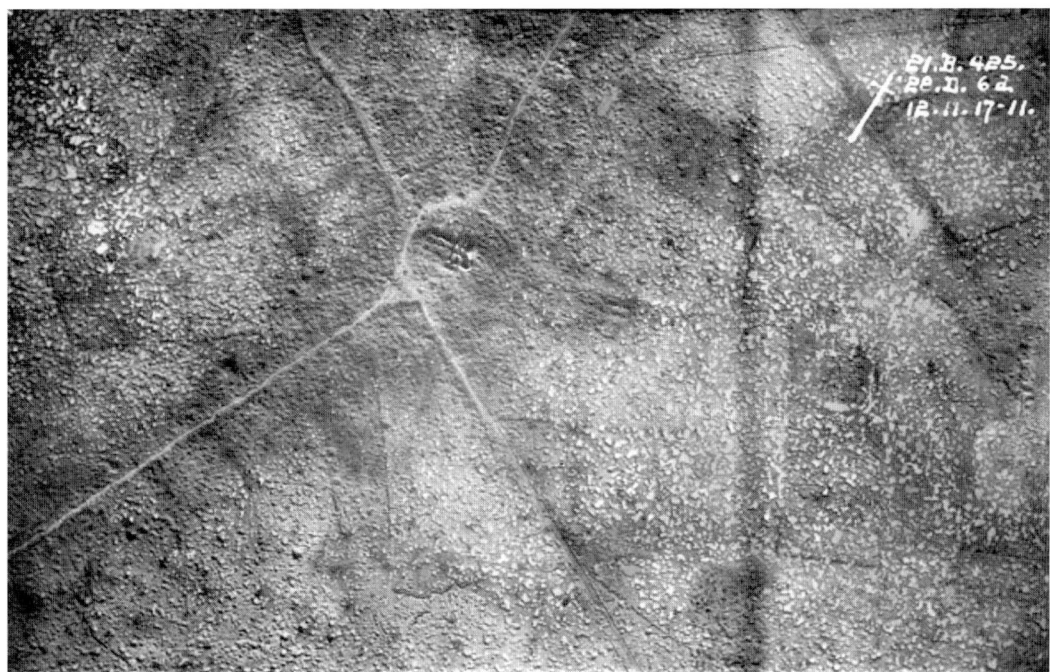

In July the next phase of that year's 'Big Push' by the Allied forces saw the Third Battle of Ypres begin. After a summer of wet weather, followed by days and weeks of heavy gunfire, the battlefield presented an almost impassable scene of devastation. In time it would be called the Battle of Passchendaele and come to represent the unnecessary slaughter of a whole generation of young men on both sides of the lines. This photo captures the scene that presented itself each day to von Richthofen and his men that summer and autumn as they flew from Markebeeke and its satellite airfields. (*Author*)

Fokker himself. He, in fact, oversaw several very public presentations and demonstration flights with von Richthofen's and Werner Voss' assistance. In this they were supported by such dignitaries as the German Chancellor Georg Michaelis, who had recently come to power, Ludendorff, General Friedrich Sixt von Arnim and Major General Fritz von Lossberg. Being seen alongside Germany's national hero would have played well for Michaelis' and the army's reputation. All of this was carefully choreographed and captured on cine film and in press photographs for home consumption. But in doing so the cameramen also captured a very tired-looking von Richthofen, with his wound still visible, clearly not the same man he had been only three months earlier.

So, in an effort to promote the new triplane and secure Fokker much bigger contracts, von Richthofen soon flew Dr.I number 102/17 operationally for the first time. Two more victories in early September soon followed. The first was an R.E.8 on 2 September, resulting in death of its observer, Walter Kember, and a wounded and captured pilot, John Madge. Then on 3 September he faced a tougher opponent in the form of Algernon Bird, a No. 46 Squadron pilot flying an outdated but still potent Sopwith Pup, to record his sixty-first victory. Bird, writing in his diary during 1927 recalled his memories of this day:

During August 1917 cine photographers captured some scenes of day to day life in JG1 in this case during a visit by Albrecht von Richthofen and Anthony Fokker. The warmth of the relationship between father and son is only too apparent. (*CD/Author*)

Kunigunde von Richthofen later recorded that Manfred arrived home on leave in a 'red plane ... which is now his own property'. (Top right and left) This was, most probably, the red Albatros C.1X two-seater seen in these two group of photographs, here apparently photographed at Hanover in the summer of 1917. The other group of four pictures captures a similar scene with the same aircraft but this time with Anthony Fokker in attendance. Wherever he went, his departures and arrivals drew audiences, with many simply wishing to see and be seen with their 'great hero'. (*CD/Author*)

In late August the first two Fokker Dr.I Triplanes arrived on the Western Front. No. 102/17 was handed over to von Richthofen by Anthony Fokker in a series of very public ceremonies. These apparently involved such dignitaries as the recently appointed German Chancellor Georg Michaelis (top right and middle left speaking to an apparently downcast von Richthofen), Ludendorff and Major General Fritz von Lossberg (bottom left). Fokker brought a cine camera with him (top left) to film some of these events. Meanwhile, Dr.I No. 103/17 was presented to Werner Voss, now leading Jasta 10 (lower right – seen here leaning into the cockpit to show a visitor the controls). Voss would die in this aircraft a short while later. (*CD/Author*)

The flight took off shortly after 6 am and having attained a height of about 4,200 metres proceeded to cross the lines to a point about 10 miles over on the German side and commenced the patrol. Normally on these occasions we were treated to a liberal dose of Archie (anti-aircraft gunfire), but on the morning in question everything appeared more than usually calm.

As far as my recollection goes we had covered our allotted beat once and had just turned to repeat the process when an enemy machine was seen some way below us and the flight commander indicated his intention of diving. I followed suit and by this time another enemy machine having appeared proceeded to attack him.

It thus became clear that we were involved in a scrap with a large number of the enemy. While chasing my particular opponent I took a glance over my shoulder to find myself being followed by two triplanes which I at once took to belong to an RNAS squadron with whom we occasionally cooperated. The next thing I knew was that I was under a fusillade from machine guns at very close quarters, my engine cut out and I got one under my right arm which momentarily knocked me out.

On recovering I found that I had got to do all I knew if I was going to stand a chance of reaching our lines. The two enemy triplanes were making wonderful shooting at me and my machine was being hit many times without number, the splinters flying from the small struts in front of the cockpit and from the instrument board. It was impossible to fly straight for more than a few moments at a time before they got their guns on me again and my progress towards our lines was very slow compared with the height I was losing for my engine was a passenger only.

It began to be quite obvious that I should not succeed in regaining our lines as I was now within a few hundred feet of the ground and looking for a place to put my machine down. I found a field in which a German fatigue party were digging trenches, in this I eventually landed hitting, I believe, a tree in the process: all this while my assailants had kept up a heavy fire whenever they could get their guns on me.

Upon my machine coming to a rest it looked as if the trench digging party were going to finish the work that their airmen had begun but fortunately for me an officer drove up in a horse and cart and took charge, taking me back to the HQ of a Kite Balloon section where I was searched, my flying kit removed and my wound dressed. This proved to be very slight.

Whether this burst of action was too much for von Hoeppner and 4th Army is unclear but von Richthofen was despatched on prolonged leave three days later, leaving von Döring again in command.

Although his mother was probably eagerly awaiting his arrival, clearly worried about his safety, Manfred was slow to arrive. The attraction of an invitation from the Duke of Saxe-Coburg Gotha to stay at his lodge – Schloss Reinhardsbrunn – where he could hunt, proved too strong to ignore. Here he remained for a while, perhaps finding the solitude comforting as well as restful. But in his absence on leave he lost two close friends

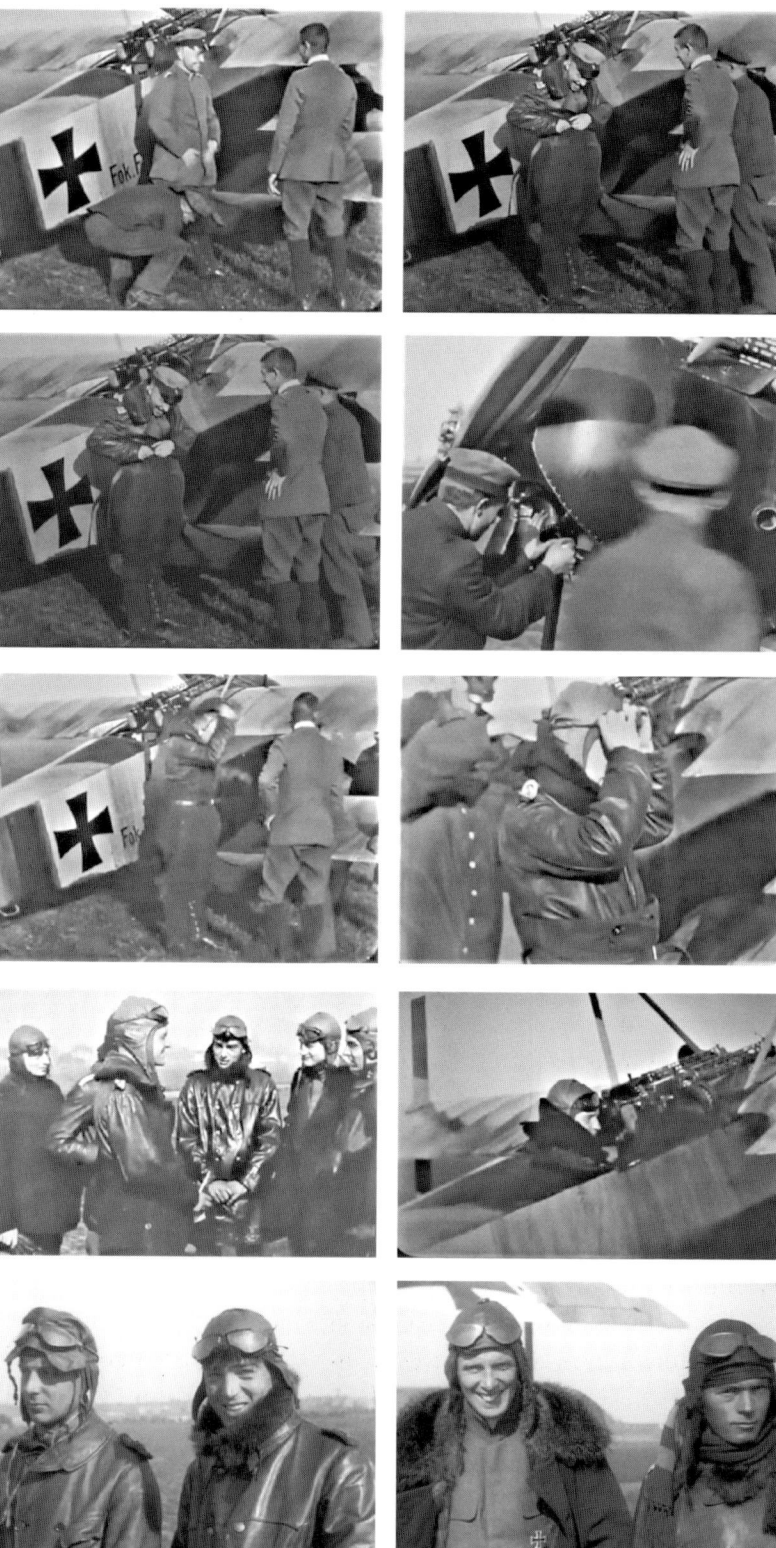

In late August a cine film was taken, possibly by Anthony Fokker, showing von Richthofen preparing for a flight in triplane No. 102/17. It was clearly staged managed, for it is far too relaxed and reveals a sense of fun that was unlikely to been the case if it was a true operational mission. Nevertheless, it does give us a rare and fascinating view of day to day life in JG1 at that time and one that found favour at home when the film was released for general viewing. The bottom photos show four of his pilots two of them 'enjoying' the moment while the other two strike rather awkward poses (Left to right – thought to be Lt Hans Karl von Linsingen, Lt Karl Meyer, Lt Gisbert Groos and Lt Eberhardt Mohnicke, if so all four appear to have survived the war). (*Author*)

– Kurt Wolff, when flying triplane No. 102/17, and, worst of all, Werner Voss in the other triplane on the 23rd September. The impact of these deaths on the slowly recovering Rittmeister are not hard to imagine.

After his brief hunting trip, Manfred arrived at Schweidnitz on the 17th September by air in, according to his mother, 'the red plane … which is now his own property'. He then brought it down on a landing strip 'filled with a crowd', which drew from his mother the brief observation that 'we had trouble, in spite of the barricades, in reaching our house'. After a few months away she clearly wished to see her son and reassure herself that he was well and coping with the strain. However, she was clearly shocked by what she found:

> Manfred's wound is deeper than I thought. With sadness I noticed that the hair on his head has grown thinner. It looks as though he has a bald head. To my horror, I found that his head wound is still far from healed. The bone still lies exposed. Every other day he goes to a local hospital to have the bandage changed. He looks ill and is irritable.

Such was her concern that during his leave she summoned up the courage to express her worries and seek to influence his thoughts:

> We walked through the garden, and now I chose to speak words I had resolved to say. 'Have done with flying, Manfred!' (He replied) 'Who should fight the war then, if we all thought that way? The soldiers in the trenches?' (I replied). 'But the soldier gets relieved from time to time and go to rest camps, while several times a day you fight dangerous duels at 5,000 metres'.
>
> Manfred became impatient. 'Would it please you if I moved to a place of safety now and rested on my laurels?'

There was, as his mother soon realised, no moving him, so all she could do was stand by, give him what support she could and watch his health deteriorate. The effects of this deterioration became only too apparent when her son was called to greet the constantly gathering crowds at their front door:

> After lunch, Manfred had scarcely lain down – his head was particularly painful today – when another group appeared. My husband had to go upstairs to wake him. A few minutes later, he appeared at the front door. He was almost unfriendly. The ovation he received did not suit him and he wasn't able to hide his bad temper despite all eyes being fixed on him. I suggested that he be friendlier on the next occasion. Manfred stormed out in an almost brusque way, his eyes narrow and hard (saying): 'If I fly over the trenches and the soldiers cheer me and I look into their faces, grey from hunger, sleeplessness and battle – then I am glad … that is my reward.'

Another event in von Richthofen's life that received wide coverage in the press and on cinema screens was a combat on 3 September in which he shot down a No. 46 Squadron Sopwith Pup piloted by Algernon Bird (upper right and middle left talking to von Richthofen, who could, apparently speak some English), who lived to tell the tale. Again Anthony Fokker was on hand and is seen seated on the fuselage beside von Richthofen (top left). (*Author*)

The next day, he left for East Prussia, to find solitude in the huge game reserve there. Here he would find himself more quickly. Here the soul of the forest would speak to him.

Manfred's return to the front on 23 October must have been accompanied by mixed emotions. Having observed the sorry state of affairs in Germany and JG I's activities, its successes and its losses, a sense of sombre reality probably prevailed. Although it was now four months since he had been wounded, its effects would still be apparent to him, as they were to his family and would soon be to his fellow pilots. Hans-Georg von der Osten recalled that:

September 1917 saw von Richthofen finally taking leave from the front to help his recovery from the wound on 6 July. After a few days' hunting at Schloss Reinhardsbrunn he returned home, to be greeted by crowds and press photographers eager to see their young hero (top left and right with his family and with Lothar, who was soon to return to action). In Manfred's absence he lost two close friends, Kurt Wolff on 15 September and Werner Voss eight days later. (Middle left) Von Richthofen dresses up for the camera and poses with Moritz. (Middle right) Reported to be Wolff's crashed Dr.I No. 102/17 initially allocated to von Richthofen. (Lower left) Wolff's funeral. (Lower right) Voss with Dr.I No. 103/17, in which he was shot down by members of No. 56 Squadron on 23 September. He was roughly buried near the site of the crash, but his grave and his remains were obliterated by gunfire shortly afterwards. (*CD/Author*)

We were pleased to welcome him back and while he seemed rested he no longer cut the robust figure of old. His spark had gone, to be replaced by a grim determination to do his duty. This was accompanied by greater concern for our welfare. While he accepted that we had to fight and face death, he sought to reduce the risks and would only let us fly if the conditions favoured us or it was absolutely necessary to do so. Although never a 'party man', he now withdrew to his quarters as soon as his duties allowed him to do so, keeping his hound close by at all times. He would often be seen walking across the fields with Moritz his sole company ... Periodically, he still attended hospital to have his head wound treated, so it was clearly still troubling him.

Any mention of old friends who had been lost clearly pained him, particularly the two most recently departed – Wolff and Voss. However, all of us found accepting the loss of friends increasingly difficult and by then we all tended to avoid close friendships. Did this help? I'm afraid not, because each loss still had the power to hurt you deeply. By 1918 the Rittmeister had faced death constantly for nearly four years and was clearly brooding badly on these issues. We all felt that such a gallant man should have been withdrawn from service in late 1917 before the inevitable happened. But his sense of duty wouldn't allow this to happen and his value seemed to be too great to the High Command for them to sanction his transfer to non-operational duties.

(Above left) The note on the back of this print simply states that this is 'Von Richthofen and an unknown aviator – November 1917'. I have no reason to doubt this. (Above right) A photo thought to have been taken in late 1917 outside the 'Officers Casino at Markebeeke' before or after a conference of fighter leaders, including Karl Bolle of Jasta 2 and Josef Mai of Jasta 5. (*CD/Author*)

On 30 October, when flying with his brother, who was forced to land with engine failure, Manfred wrote off triplane No. 114/17 when landing near Lothar's aircraft. This photo is thought to show No. 114/17 later that day, although without sight of the aircraft's number or other evidence confirmation of this is impossible. (*PC*)

And so Manfred returned to the Western Front recognisably unfit to fly again and facing the last major Allied campaign of the year. Before this attack had begun he flew a number of times without apparent success and did not mention suffering from nausea or dizziness as a result. However, on 30 October 1917 he was flying with his brother when, according to JG I's War Diary they, 'made emergency landings at 9.50 am near Zilverberg, both uninjured. The Rittmeister's machine was totally demolished, the other machine undamaged.'

As the winter approached, the British attack began with the hope of achieving the breakthrough that had so far eluded them that year, at a cost in lives that many thought bordered on the unsustainable. The village of Passchendaele had finally been taken after nearly four months of unendurable losses, so bringing the Third Battle of Ypres to an end, but still the British commanders wanted more. Now the battle switched to Cambrai in the hope that the drier ground there, a change of tactics and the mass deployment of tanks, might bring them the major success they craved. A short, sharp barrage, a sea of tanks advancing over no man's land, cleaving a path through German defences, and Royal Flying Corps aircraft undertaking ground strafing raids, succeeded and soon a long-desired breakthrough was at hand. Sadly, insufficient reserves were forthcoming to push home the advantage and soon the German army counter-attacked in strength and most of the gains so gallantly achieved early in the battle were lost.

With a victory of sorts at Passchendaele, the British turned their attention, in late November, on a thrust towards Cambrai. Here, for the first time, tanks were used in their hundreds and these quickly broke through the German defences. But the Allies failed to exploit the huge advantage they gained and a counter-attack soon drove them back towards their jumping off positions. JG I was actively involved in the defence of Cambrai and would have been only too familiar with Bourlon and Quarry Woods, as seen here from 3,000m, the furthest the British advanced. (*Author*)

As the British pressed forward, JG I were hastily transferred to 2nd Army's front to help counter the threat, but were hindered in their attacks by fog, rain, low, thick cloud and high winds. Nevertheless, they engaged the enemy when they could and on the 23rd September sent down three of their number, including one by Manfred flying Albatros D.V No. 4693/17, a DH.5, and a Bristol F.2b by his brother. Three days later, when flying with Lothar and Leutnant Gusman, Manfred repeated this feat, sending down a 41 Squadron S.E.5a 'in flames in the vicinity of the Steinbruch Forest'.

All this was observed by Anthony Fokker from close quarters during his occasional visits to JG I that autumn and winter, who wrote of Manfred that:

He had a great deal of executive work to attend to as well as his daily combat flights. Secretaries raced about, and orderlies came and went all day … He was an excellent teacher, and young pilots who showed exceptional skill were sent to his staffel to get experience … Richthofen would gather his officers together for a conference and a discussion of tactics. Occasionally he would censure pilots who were too aggressive,

Following the successful arrival of the Sopwith Triplane on the Western Front, German manufacturers sought to develop their own version. Fokker, with his Dr.I, seems to have led the field with Pfalz not far behind. In December 1917 von Richthofen, as these pictures reveal, visited their works at Speyer to test fly this triplane and seems to have concluded that it offered few, if any, advantages over the Fokker. (*Author*)

or too willing to pull away before a battle was over. He was, perhaps, not so much liked as admired, but the respect other pilots had for him was unbounded.

Proud though he was, the acclaim for his achievements gave him no particular pleasure. He was not interested in publicity, and though he received letters by the ton from all sorts of people, he cared little for fan mail. When he was around, parties were never wild, for the other pilots felt constrained in the presence of their chief.

With the Battle for Cambrai coming to an end, hastened by ever worsening weather, all became quiet on the Western Front for a time. This allowed Manfred to focus more fully on other duties, including test flying a new Pfalz-produced triplane in December at their Speyer works. He then returned to JG I for Christmas, where he was joined by his father, who must have been greatly relieved to see his sons surviving all the perils they had faced, but undoubtedly still worrying incessantly about their ability to survive in such a bloody war.

Shortly afterwards Manfred travelled home to Schweidnitz to see his mother for what seems to have been the last time. She, having seen a general disenchantment with the country's leaders and the war growing all around her, sought to counsel her weary, troubled son:

We sat in my husband's study. Manfred says that he will now be sent more often to munition factories – to meet striking workers. When [on an earlier visit] he arrived they all rushed towards him and he spoke to them. He made it clear to them just how important their work was … Then some went back to their machines, but, perhaps, not for long. In this respect he was rather pessimistic.

Together we looked at photographs that Manfred had brought with him. A very fine photo showed a group of young flying officers. In the centre was Manfred … 'What has become of him?' I pointed to the first. 'Fallen.' I indicated the second. 'Also dead,' and his voice sounded harsh. 'Ask no further questions – they are all dead …'

Go no further, said a voice within me. Someone stands before me, who is so near death, that it stares him in the face more than once a day – and he is your child – then be careful and tactful with every word … So one remains silent, to appreciate the moment, and enjoy the presence of the other.

I found Manfred very changed … he was taciturn, aloof, almost unapproachable; every one of his words seemed to come from an unknown place. Why this change? The thought haunted me … I think he has seen death too often.

It is easy to read too much into a portrait, nevertheless, this picture taken in the winter of 1917–18 does, to my mind capture a resolute but war-weary young man. When viewing photos of those who were fighting, one common feature, often commented upon, was their 'thousand yard stare'. Bearing in mind that Manfred had been in almost continuous action since August 1914, this is not surprising. But here we also have a man still recovering from a serious head wound and suffering the long-term consequences of this trauma. (CD)

'Actually [he said], there is really is no point in it anymore.' These were words of a troubled spirit and would not be dismissed [from my mind]. I closed my eyes as if I wanted to rest, though none of his actions escaped me. How hard his features had become … Something painful lay around his eyes and brow. Was it a presentment of the future – the serious outcome of the war he had feared throwing a long shadow over him? Or was it only an after-effect of the deep head wound he had suffered in the summer?

Certainly, he had never complained, but for a time it had stripped him of all his strength. He had looked different; very wretched and sensitive … that was now past, but solemnity, reserve, dignity and an enigma had taken its place. I have never seen Manfred so. I did not know him this way.

The serious mood Manfred left behind remained with us in the house. Cares, thoughts, despondency – evil spirits.

Kunigunde was clearly concerned about her son. She had always been aware of a certain fatalism in his character brought on by war, but this was different, as she clearly realised.

As he entered the last few months of his life, von Richthofen tended to isolate himself more from his family and his fellow pilots, seeking some solace in the company of his dog. However, there has been speculation over the years of a romance, seemingly confirmed by his mother during the 1920s and 1930s. After such a long period of time this is unlikely to ever be more than a charming tale or simply wishful thinking, unless, of course, some concrete evidence emerges. Both Charles Donald and Pasquale Carisella were aware of the rumours and remained uncommitted on this point, although each acquired a photo of this anonymous young lady, they both said, from the von Richthofen family and were given the impression that she and Manfred were, at least, correspondents. If so, it is reassuring to think that he may have gained some solace from such a relationship in such a challenging period of his young life. (*CD/PC*)

Now the stresses and strains he bore, plus the lasting effects of his wounds were pressing down on him, increasingly stripping him of any peace of mind. This was battle fatigue at its worst, bringing on a sense of despondency and melancholy. She saw, without any doubt, that he should retire from the fray, but also realised that his all-pervading sense of duty would not allow him to do so and her inability to say anything haunted her for the rest of her life.

# Part 6

# January to April 1918

Winter in northern Europe does not lend itself to fighting wars and tends to bring any conflict to a temporary halt. The killing still goes on, but on a diminished scale. In this case the British were exhausted by their sacrifices of 1917 and required time to build up their strength again. The Germans too were at full stretch and needed reinforcements. But the pressures they were under were, if anything, greater because of the gradual build-up of American forces in Europe and the threat this posed to the country's survival.

When visiting Berlin that January Manfred would have been only too aware of the dire shortages of food and the numerous queues for anything that was on offer. He may also have been aware of the growing anti-war movement and the increasing threat of

The winter of 1917–18 saw the arrival of von Richthofen's autobiography and a revival of interest in the life of *Der Rote Kampfflieger*. Sales of the book were brisk and photographers and reporters were soon beating a path to his door. Today 'photo shoots' are part and parcel of being a celebrity, but in early 1918, when Manfred and his brother posed for this group of photographs, the concept was still a new one. Judging by their expressions on this and the adjoining page, it seems to have been a tiresome business, with the only sign of any humour or warmth contained in Manfred's downward stare at his dog. (*Author*)

Germany in the winter of 1918 was a far from united country. Huge losses, plus shortages of food and raw material, were beginning to strip bare the populations' desire or ability to continue fighting. On his visits to Berlin in January von Richthofen would have seen for himself, as the pictures above and on the adjoining page reveal, food kitchens seeking to provide a most basic level of subsistence for huge numbers of people and the constant search for any foodstuffs. There were also strikes in essential industries, plus mass anti-war and anti-government protests to observe that month. For such a well-ordered, authoritarian society these were indeed worrying trends. (*Author*)

In early January 1918, due to their status as national heroes, the von Richthofen brothers were ordered to attend the Peace negotiations with the Russians at Brest-Litovsk. They were among the party to greet the enemy delegation at the local station and then the opening ceremony. (Above) It is said that Manfred is in the centre of this group, partially hidden by the raised arm of the Russian in the black coat. (Below) A note with this photograph suggests that 'the brothers are at the back of the German delegation on the left hand side of the picture. Manfred appears to be standing on something to allow him to peer over the top, with Lothar partly hidden to his right'. This may be so but confirmation so long after the event is unlikely. Nevertheless, they were both there somewhere. (*CD/Author*)

civil disobedience in support of this cause. In such circumstances the role of national heroes, whose example might encourage the continued acceptance of the appalling losses, was even more important. And so, in the months before von Richthofen's death, the exploitation grew apace, with little regard for his well-being or, it seems, his survival. As a good, obedient soldier he had no choice but to acquiesce, no matter what the cost, with his newsworthiness being fostered and exploited by newsreels, the publication of his memoirs and high-profile public appearances whenever possible.

The first of those took place immediately after Christmas when he was ordered with his brother to attend the opening stages of peace talks with a Russian delegation at Brest-Litovsk, a place Manfred had often flown over earlier in the war. Here the German contingent contrived a show of strength to intimidate the enemy. So, the highly publicised von Richthofen brothers were included in a party glistening with a cross section of senior officers decked out in their highly burnished gold braid and uniforms. But in putting on this show of strength, led by Crown Prince Leopold, Supreme Commander of the German forces in the east, they failed to realise that Russia's new leaders could not be bullied because the struggle for power in their country was significantly more important to them than continued war against Germany. So Manfred and Lothar, after being photographed at the station greeting the Russians and attending the opening sessions, were released and escaped for a time to the tsar's hunting lodge in the Bialowieza Forest to shoot stag, before returning to Germany.

Then, a few days later, Manfred received this written instruction:

19 January: Rittmeister Freihher von Richthofen ordered to Berlin-Adlershof until further notice.

Perhaps stung by von Richthofen's criticisms of the poor standard of fighter aircraft in his letter of July 1917, the *Inspekteur der Flieger* (Idflieg) decided to hold a series of fighter trials to test all candidates for future front-line service. It was an event that would involve a number of fighter aces, including von Richthofen, who would be given the power to decide which of the competitors was best.

On 20 January these men and the manufacturers, including Fokker, Albatros, Junker, DFW, Kondor, Pfalz and Roland, gathered together, with more than thirty new or modified types of aircraft to test and compare. From the beginning it was agreed that pilots had to choose two aircraft from the group, one with a Mercedes in-line engine and the other rotary powered. Complete standardisation was thought by those in charge to be too restrictive because it limited operational flexibility and so more than one winner was deemed necessary.

Fokker prepared for these trials very carefully and presented nine different models for the pilots to consider, including the V.II biplane and two Dr.Is with more powerful engines. By 12 February all the testing and assessments were complete. For von Richthofen there was a clear winner in the Fokker V.11, with the Roland D.VIa as runner-up. While in the rotary engine class he thought the Fokker V.13, powered by a Siemens-Halske

(Top left and right and lower left) Von Richthofen looking relaxed during the fighter trials at Adlershof in January 1918. (Lower right) The Fokker V.11 (soon to be designated the D.VII) seems to have been the unanimous choice of the pilots involved in these evaluations, undoubtedly encouraged by Manfred. (*CD/Author*)

SH.III engine, to be the 'best all round type … easy to fly, very manoeuvrable, and similar to the V.11'.

With Manfred's all-important support assured, contracts were signed and, in April, the first few D.VIIs, as the V.11s became known, reached the Western Front, soon demonstrating their superiority to aircrew on both sides of the lines. Sadly, their primary advocate would not get the chance to enjoy this dominance.

By mid-February von Richthofen was back with his Geschwader and soon heavily involved in preparing his pilots for a forthcoming German offensive code-named Michael, to be fought over the old Somme battlefield. Secrecy was essential, with preparations taking place, whenever possible, at night. However, with British reconnaissance aircraft operating in some strength there was always a chance that they might spot the telltale signs of the coming battle. So a strengthening of German fighter squadrons operating in the area was to be expected, with JG I taking the lead.

In the weeks leading up to the battle the weather favoured the German army, in so far as it was frequently foggy, with rain and clouds also helping to screen the build-up of

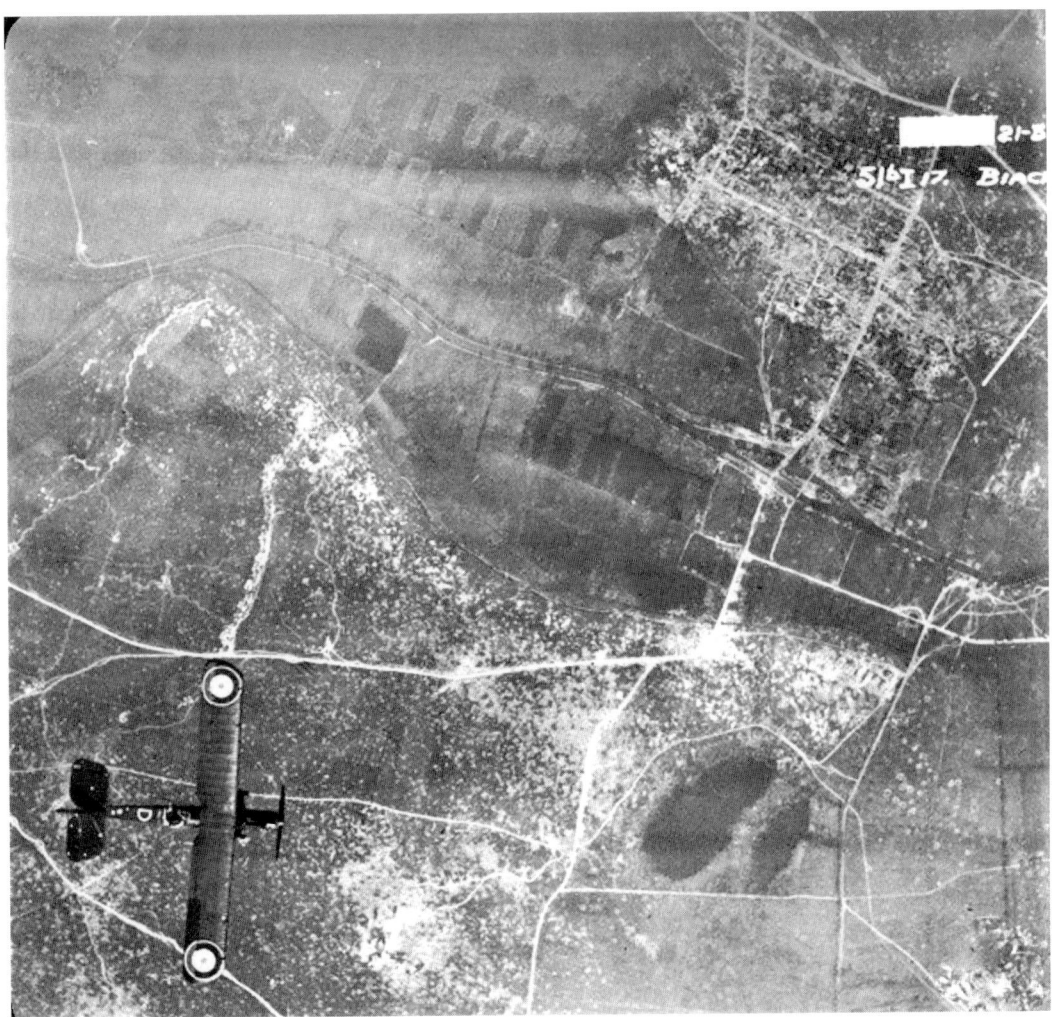

The air war on the Western Front was in early 1918, if anything, more hotly contested than at any other time during the conflict. After its setbacks in the first half of 1917, the RFC were by March 1918 in the ascendancy and the German air force on the back foot. With its proliferation of good pilots, a great responsibility fell on von Richthofen and JG I's shoulders in particular to achieve some sort of temporary superiority whenever and wherever required. (Above) A scene typical of early 1918 – a DH.4 undertaking reconnaissance duties. (*Author*)

arms. Some flying was possible, but successes were rare until early March. There was a Bristol F.2b on 16 February, a 'French biplane' on 8 March and a Sopwith two days later. Yet in the process JG I sustained an irritatingly high number of casualties – one killed, six seriously wounded and one becoming a prisoner of war,

If he flew during these fallow weeks, Manfred failed to add to his score, then, finally on 11 March, with the arrival of better weather, JG 1 had some success when two enemy aircraft were shot down; one credited to his brother, the other to Vizefeldwebel Scholtz. The 12 March was even better with five enemy aircraft and two captive balloons destroyed, one of them, a Bristol F.2b from No. 62 Squadron, forced down by Manfred

During the last few weeks of his life, as Germany prepared its final offensives of the war, von Richthofen and his brother were photographed frequently at the airfields occupied by JG 1 as the pictures above and on the next two pages reveal. After a quiet winter they were newsworthy again. These pictures capture the brothers together and separately, with fellow pilots, in the few weeks before Lothar was seriously wounded on 13 March. In 1918 JG I moved from 4th Army control to the 2nd Army, for whom Major Wilhelm Haehnelt was, as Kofl, von Richthofen's first point of contact. He can be seen in the second to last photograph in this group, to Manfred's right, talking to Lothar. (*CD/Author*)

behind German lines, where the crew were soon captured, to become his sixty-fourth victim. Later, as a mark of respect for the observer who had put up a strong fight despite being badly wounded, Manfred sent half a dozen cigars and his best wishes for a speedy recovery.

Manfred repeated this success on 13 March, shortly after his brother was seen to crash his triplane near Awoingt, where JG I had moved at the end of February to be closer to the action. Von Richthofen visited his brother in hospital and quickly sent a telegram to his mother letting her know what had happened, followed by a letter in which he wrote:

> Thank God he is doing well [having suffered severe facial injuries]. I visit him daily. So, please, do not worry about anything. He is doing well.
>
> His nasal bones have already healed, only the mandible has been cracked, but all his teeth have been saved. He has a large gash over his right eye, but the eye itself has not been injured. Some blood vessels have burst on his right knee and the left leg from the calf muscle down, similarly there has been some bleeding.
>
> Blood that he coughed up was not a result of any internal injury, rather it had been swallowed in the crash. He is in hospital in Cambrai and hopes to be up and about in fourteen days. He is very sorry that he cannot be with us now [with the offensive due to begin shortly].

Now without the reassuring presence of his brother, Manfred may have found the pressure he had to bear growing daily more intolerable. And all the time the demand for more news, to feed the public, propagandists and the press alike, did not abate. In fact, the appearance of *Der Rote Kampfflieger* only made the clamour grow louder, with VIPs and reporters visiting the front to meet and interview him. One can't imagine a more trying existence for a fit person, let alone someone suffering the effects of war weariness and poor mental health even before the big offensive had begun.

To help understand his thoughts at this time we have Manfred's own words to help us. At about this time he wrote:

> Hanging from the ceiling of my 'dugout' is a lamp I created as a conversation piece from the engine of an aircraft I shot down. I mounted small lamps in each cylinder and when I lie awake at night and let the light burn, Lord knows the chandelier looks wonderful and strange. When I lie this way, I have much to consider … The battle now taking place on all fronts has become very grim – there is nothing left of the 'spirited, cheery war', as it was called in the beginning. Now we must fight against despair and arm ourselves so that the enemy cannot invade our country.
>
> I am in wretched spirits after each aerial battle. This, no doubt, is an after-effect of my head wound. When I set foot on the ground after a flight, I go to my quarters and do not want to see anyone or hear anything. I think of this war as it really is, not as people at home imagine it, with a Hoorah! And a cheer. It is very serious and very grim.

(Top and middle) Lothar von Richthofen's badly damaged Dr.I, No. 454/17, after he had crash-landed following an encounter with 'a crowd of Englishmen', as he later related. He smashed his head against his machine guns and suffered severe facial injuries that kept him away from the front until July. (Below) A few days later Manfred was photographed visiting Jasta 5 and is seen here chatting to, among others, Oberleutnant Richard Flashar, No. 5's commanding officer. (*CD/Author*)

Lothar's loss, albeit temporarily, in March was just one of the casualties JG I and the other fighter squadrons had to bear that month as the German offensive got under way. On 6 March, Leutnant Erich Bahr of Jasta 11 was killed. (Left and below) Here von Richthofen, (immediately behind the cross the pastor is holding in the upper picture) leads the mourners on 10 March and then walks slowly past the open grave. (Second from bottom) On the 10 March Leutnant Wilhelm Gürke of Jasta 5 went down in flames and Manfred attended his funeral (far left), flying there in an Albatros D.V on this occasion and seen here bidding Richard Flashar and others farewell (bottom picture). (*PC/Author*)

On 17 March – greeting von Hoeppner during the general's inspection of JG I that day. (*CD*)

The release of Germany's painstakingly assembled forces on 21 March must have come as a relief to Manfred and his many comrades in the front line after the stalemate of winter. After a short, sharp barrage, German troops pushed forward en masse, benefiting from a thick fog that lay across the battlefield. The enemy quickly fell back; thousands being killed or taken prisoner along the way.

It soon became apparent that they had chosen a most opportune moment to strike. After the strain of almost continuous offensives since Loos in late 1915, the British Army was at a low ebb, could do little to stem the assault and needed time to muster its strength before it could do anything but retreat towards Amiens. However, by slow degrees, reinforcements arrived and by the middle of April this first and most important phase of Ludendorff's programme of offensives had stalled, falling well short of Amiens let alone reaching the coast and breaking the enemy's will to resist. While this happened, the Royal Flying Corps and Royal Naval Air Service, which had joined together to become the RAF on 1 April, vigorously resisted the enemy; low-level attacks on German troops, when the weather allowed, proving particularly effective. So, it was hardly surprising that such aggression was met by an equally strong reaction from von Richthofen and his fellow pilots.

To the general public reading of von Richthofen's ever-growing score – reaching seventy-four by the end of March 1918 – the glory of the previous April and May seemed to have returned. But the man they idolised was now greatly changed from the hero of those heady days. He was now haunted by death, as became only too clear to Peter Lampel when visiting JG I on one of several sojourns to the front he made in early April for *Der Flieger*.

JG I during the Michael offensive when the unit moved south to counter the threat posed by the enemy over the Somme. (Top) Jasta 11's triplanes photographed at Awoingt when the March offensive began. As German troops rapidly gained ground, the Jasta had to move forward to remain close to the action. (Middle) Triplanes of Jastas 6 and 10 lined up at Léchelle, where they were based from late March. An observer scans the sky through binoculars for any enemy aircraft. (Bottom) Von Richthofen (fourth from the left) strides towards his partly red-painted Dr.I, No. 127/17, at Léchelle, a stepladder waiting to help him climb into the cockpit encumbered by his heavy flying kit. (*CD/Author*)

On 2 April Lampel happened to meet and speak to von Richthofen over lunch shortly after he had shot down his seventy-fifth victim – an R.E.8 from 52 Squadron flown by 19-year-old Welshman Ernest Jones and his observer Robert Francis, a 24-year-old bank clerk from Bristol. In his combat report he simply recorded that:

> At around 12.30 I attacked an RE 8 at an altitude of 800 metres, directly below the clouds, above the wood of Moreuil. As my adversary only saw me late, I managed to approach within 50 metres. From a range of ten metres I fired at him until he began to burn. When the flames appeared I was only five metres away from him. I could see how the observer and pilot were leaning out of their plane trying to escape the flames. The machine did not explode in the air but gradually burnt away. It fell out of control to the ground, where it exploded and burnt to ashes.

When von Richthofen spoke to Lampel the image of these men's terrible death, by fire, was fixed in his mind. A murderer would feel no shame, but Manfred's conscience was clearly pricked by what he had seen close to, even though he had sent many other men to their deaths before.

And so the battles continued to rage in April without let-up, and with increasingly less chance of success. JG I moved from Awoingt to Léchelle, a recently vacated British airfield, where Lampel had met von Richthofen. They were then placed under the direct authority of 'Army High Command to be deployed at the focal point of the battle', according to the War Diary. Then, on 12 April, they moved again, this time to an airfield on rising ground above the village of Cappy. Here they overlooked the Somme as it wound its way past Corbie and Villers-Bretonneux, where the Germans had been fought to a standstill by the enemy with Amiens still 14km or so away.

The weather, as much as anything, dictated the ebb and flow of the air battle and on many days that April, rain, low cloud and high winds ruled out a great deal of operational flying, or at best made interceptions very difficult to achieve. But on 6 April JG I claimed ten victories, nine of them Sopwith Camels, with one of them shot down by von Richthofen. His seventy-sixth victim was the 22-year-old Sydney Philip Smith, an experienced combat pilot from 46 Squadron, who was brought up in Aldershot and whose body was consumed by fire and the explosion that followed the crash north-east of Villers-Bretonneux. Next day he repeated the trick twice by destroying what he recorded as an S.E.5, to which he added inverted commas as though unsure of the type, and a SPAD, though the RFC were no longer operating these on the Western Front, although the French were. Later research suggests that it may have been a 73 Squadron Sopwith Camel flown by the 22-year-old Ronald Adams.

Bad weather and the transfer to Cappy curtailed von Richthofen's flying activities, but on 20 April he was again in action and scored a double victory by shooting down two Sopwith Camels from 3 Squadron in rapid succession. First of all, he despatched No. 3's 23-year-old commanding officer, Major Richard Raymond-Barker MC, whose body was consumed by flames. Then he turned his attention towards another Camel piloted

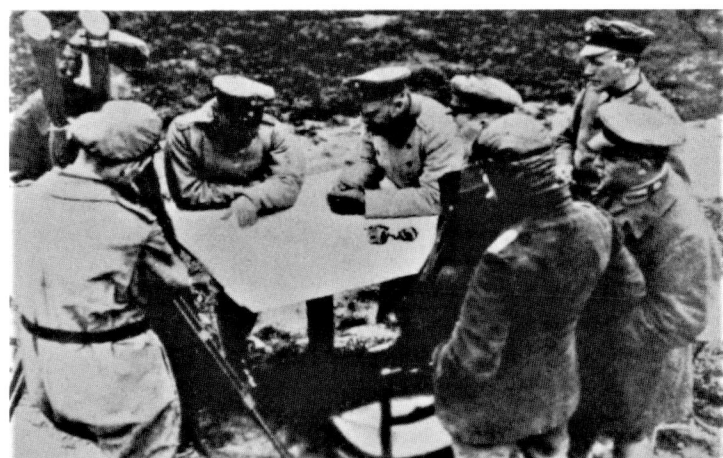

Wartime flying can involve much waiting around, often in flying kit, an airfield for the enemy to appear or for conditions to improve to allow missions to go ahead, as the top left photo of von Richthofen and another unidentified officer reveals. There would also be frequent briefings taking place (top right) as shown here with von Richthofen, fourth from the right, studying a map of the front with his men. And sometimes (lower photo) it was simply a matter of hanging around the unit's offices chatting, smoking, playing with pets and simply finding a way to pass the time (von Richthofen is fourth from the left – a photo possibly taken in April). (*CD/Author*)

by the Rhodesian-born David Lewis, who survived the encounter to be taken prisoner, although his aircraft also burned.

Very quickly news of his seventy-ninth and eightieth successes reached his mother, thanks to the good offices of the 'ever courteous editor of the *Rundschau*'. Having received this news on 21 April she was seized by:

(Top left) This photo is thought to show the all-red Dr.I No. 425/17, in which von Richthofen died. (Top right) Sydney Smith von Richthofen's seventy-sixth victim shot down and killed over Villers-Bretonneux on 6 April. (Middle) Charles Donald wrote on this print, 'Cappy a few days before von Richthofen's death. Triplane now with repainted national markings. MvR third from the right.' I have no reason to doubt this summary. (Bottom) Thought to be JG1's airfield at Cappy. (*CD/PC/Author*)

(Top) Von Richthofen chats to some of his pilots in front of an unidentified triplane. Charles Donald, when sending me this negative, wrote, 'MvR at Cappy 20th or 21st April' (*CD*). (Lower left) Von Richthofen's seventy-ninth confirmed victim, Major Richard Raymond-Barker MC, No. 3 Squadron's commanding officer and a six-victory ace. (Lower right) Within minutes of his seventy-ninth victory, von Richthofen's eightieth went down, another Camel, flown by 19-year-old David Lewis. (*Author*)

A great and joyous excitement. I went outside and danced in the garden ... A longing for peace ran through my heart. Eighty aerial victories – a dizzying achievement. It must be enough now. Behind every summit yawns an abyss ... The sky became overcast, hard gusts of wind heralded a storm ... The sight depressed me ... I don't know why I am so pensive.

The next day a telegram arrived from Albrecht, simply stating that, 'Manfred is living in English hands.' Inevitably she must have wondered what had happened, but sustained by the thought he was safe, although a prisoner of war. And for a time his comrades in France knew as little as she did, even though some had witnessed the events surrounding his 'capture'. Three of them, Karl Bodenschatz and Leutnants Richard Wenzl and Hans Joachim Wolff, later recorded their memories of that day's events and what follows draws together these recollections.

On 21 April JG I's pilots assembled early on the airfield at Cappy, although low cloud and mist ensured there would be no flying until conditions improved. While they waited, von Richthofen joined in the fun and games of his young men. One can only assume that

The daily scene that greeted JG I's pilots in April 1918 – the Somme battlefield focussing on the Germans' last desperate thrust towards Villers-Bretonneux (in the foreground with Cappy away to the left) and Amiens beyond. This photograph was taken on an unusually clear day, because that April mist, rain and low clouds over this region made flying, and ground recognition, much more difficult. (*Author*)

(Top) A question has been raised over the date this photograph of von Richthofen was taken. Richard Wenzl, who apparently took the picture, recorded it being taken on 21 April, although another source suggests the 18 April. Either way it records Manfred with his dog watched by a fellow pilot, thought to be Erich Loewenhardt, in the days or hours before his death. (Lower left and right) Two photographs recorded as showing the all-red Dr.I, No. 425/17, in which von Richthofen died. (*CD/Author*)

his success the previous day had cheered him. Added to this, he would soon depart on a much-needed period of leave to the Black Forest to hunt, accompanied by Hans Wolff, with whom he seems to have forged a close bond.

After waiting around for a couple of hours, a wind blowing from the east, coupled to a rising temperature, gradually thinned the mist, making any activity over the front more visible. A phone call from a forward observer reporting the enemy taking to the air was received and von Richthofen ordered his men to prepare for departure.

Some of JG I's pilots who were flying with von Richthofen on the morning of 21 April when his red triplane was forced to land behind enemy lines. (Top left to right) Leutnant Richard Wenzl (nearest the cockpit) and Vizefeldwebel Edfgra Sholtz. (Middle left to right) Leutnant Wolfram von Richthofen (Manfred's recently arrived cousin) and Leutnant Hans Joachim Wolff, with his pet dog. (Bottom left to right) Wolff again but in his Triplane and Walter Karjus, who lost a hand earlier in the war and managed with a prosthetic limb. (*CD/Author*)

The Somme Valley, with Morlancourt Ridge in the background, as it appeared a few weeks after von Richthofen's death. On 21 April he chased a No. 209 Squadron Sopwith Camel, flown by Lieutenant Wilfred May, along the valley. As he did so he himself was subject to attack by Captain Roy Brown of the same squadron, then passed over an area to the right, in which Australian forces were heavily dug in and were able to bring a number of machine guns to bear on the red triplane. Von Richthofen, suddenly becoming aware of the danger he was in, turned and climbed the ridge and was struck by a bullet, probably fired from the ground, and crash-landed to the right on the ridge. (*CD*)

Very quickly two flights left the ground, one of which von Richthofen led with his newly arrived cousin, Wolfram, in attendance, along with Walter Karjus, Wolff and Edgar Scholtz. They quickly gained height and spotted seven Sopwith Camels below them on the German side of the lines and another seven above, some of which then dropped down to attack a group of fighters from Jasta 5 near Sailly le Sec. Then one or two, Wolff wasn't sure which, fell on von Richthofen's flight and a general melee developed, in which Wolff occasionally spotted his leader's red triplane. While he and Karjus were fighting three Camels, von Richthofen appeared aiming at one of the enemy aircraft, then dived away in a westerly direction.

As he disengaged from the battle for a few moments, Wolff saw the Rittmeister's triplane at an 'extremely low height over the Somme near Corbie and instinctively shook my head and wondered why he was pursuing an opponent so far over the lines'. Suddenly Wolff was attacked and was forced to defend himself again. When free from the attentions of this Camel pilot he looked again for von Richthofen without success. Suspecting that something had happened to him, he and Karjus circled around at 900m

The scene on Morlancourt Ridge shortly after von Richthofen was brought down captured in a life-size diorama constructed at the Omaka Aviation Heritage Centre in New Zealand and photoshopped to add the sky. As soon as it was known who the pilot was, souvenir hunting began and the aircraft was slowly stripped down. At the same time, many of von Richthofen's personal possessions were removed. He is shown in the mock-up as wearing light brown overalls, although several sections of material held by the author suggest the colour to be closer to dark grey. (*Author*)

hoping that he would soon reappear and return with them. But it wasn't to be and when turning for home Wolff thought he spotted 'a small (red) machine on the ground that had not been there before'.

Perhaps they hoped their leader would be at Cappy when they returned, but worry soon turned to a deeply felt concern when they discovered he was missing. Bodenschatz quickly ordered some of the pilots to the scene to investigate Wolff's report. At the same time, he began telephoning observation units nearer the front to find out if they had seen or knew anything. Finally, a communication arrived from a Leutnant Fabian, an artillery observer, possibly in a tethered balloon, which simply reported that, 'Red triplane landed on hill near Corbie … Passenger has not left the aircraft.' And so their worst fears were realised and only awaited some word from the enemy in confirmation of von Richthofen's fate. This seems to have come on 22 April when German military intelligence picked up a British message, or on 23 April when a *Reuters* report, saying that von Richthofen had been killed and buried with full military honours, was intercepted.

It was news his parents had dreaded to hear for a very long time and now the worst had happened. Within days they were surrounded by visitors eager to offer their condolences, while telegrams and letters arrived from all over Germany from monarchs, politicians, military leaders, fellow pilots, friends and members of the general public. Newspapers in

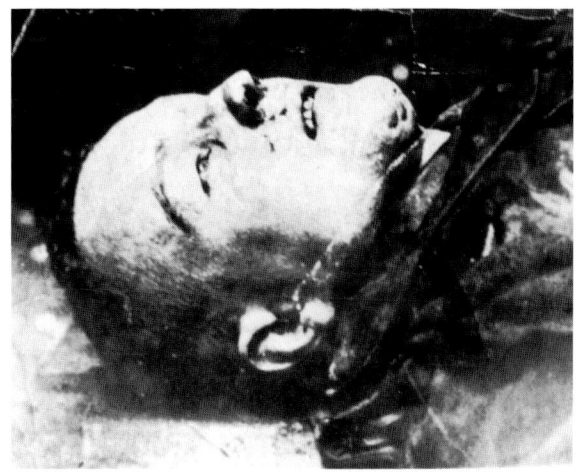

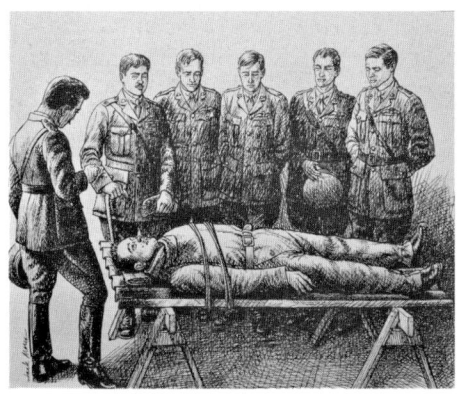

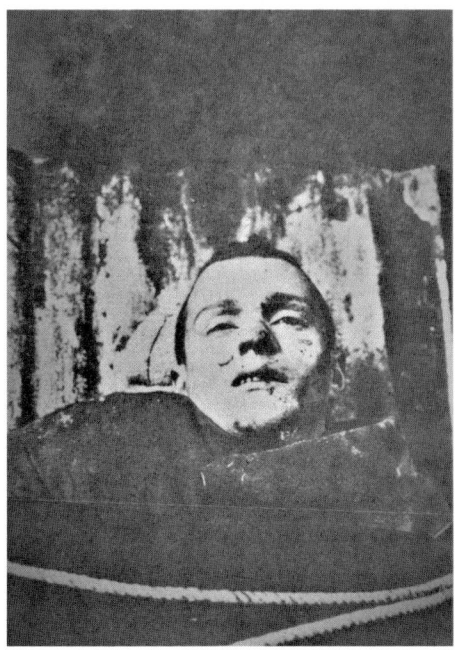

Artist Jack Moses captured the crash scene (above left) as von Richthofen's body was searched for any papers including identification. Later on, (middle left) at Bertangles, Moses records the scene when von Richthofen's body had been tied to a sheet of corrugated metal and was being viewed by a number of Allied pilots. After that he was photographed, as shown here, and then examined by doctors, including (above) Colonel George Barber, Deputy Director of Medical Services, to determine exactly how he may have died. (*JM/Author*)

To the surprise of some, von Richthofen was given a full military funeral, including a gun salute, on 22 April. In a war when most dead were consumed by gunfire, were allowed to rot on the battlefield or, at best, were simply buried in mass or hastily dug graves in shell holes, this was indeed unusual. However, by this time *Der Rote Kampfflieger* was nearly as well-known in enemy lands as in Germany, so was treated as a gallant, fallen foe. The photogrpahs above and on the adjoining page capture the scene on that day. (*CD/PC/Author*)

Germany, ever eager for a good story, were soon covered in headlines and photographs about the tragic loss. And in death even the enemy paid homage to a gallant foe, as newspaper coverage and his funeral soon revealed.

Part 7

# Aftermath

In the weeks and months following von Richthofen's death the final battles of the war raged across France and Belgium. After a series of offensives, the German army was spent and the country was on the edge of civil war, with its population near starvation. In the west US troops were arriving in ever greater numbers, reinforcing the Allies both physically and psychologically, and together they finally began to push the invaders back towards their borders. A final defeat, and the ignominy of foreign soldiers marching on Berlin, was allayed by a hastily agreed Armistice and finally the guns fell silent on the Western Front. To some this was an occasion for celebrations, but most were too shattered by the holocaust to do more than grieve for the millions of dead and the millions of men whose minds and bodies had been irrevocably damaged by all they had been asked to do for their countries.

The von Richthofen family were luckier than some in having only lost one young man, but this was little compensation and the grief his parents felt over a much-loved son was surely overpowering. So it is, perhaps, understandable that Albrecht survived his son by only two years, dying when only 60 worn out by the war and grief. And, if anything Lothar suffered even more, reportedly seeing his absence from the front, recovering from wounds at a hospital in Dusseldorf, as contributing factor to Manfred's death. He later

A living hero can inspire and encourage many to continue fighting and suffering; a dead hero only acts as a reminder of personal losses and the depleted state of one's own life. And so it was with von Richthofen, whose death was followed by an outpouring of emotion, accompanied by many headlines and pictures (above left). In Berlin, during May a service of remembrance was held (above right) attended by the great and the good, with Manfred's parents and siblings forced to bear their grief in public. (*Author*)

(Above left) Oberleutnant Wilhelm Reinhard, as von Richthofen's nominated successor, assumed command of JG I on 22 April 1918. However, in July 1918, when attending fighter trials at Adlershof and flying a Dornier-Zeppelin D.I prototype he was killed when the top wing broke free while pulling out of a dive. The Dornier's previous pilot had been Hermann Göring (above right), who, as luck would have it, was then chosen to lead JG I, taking command on 8 July until the end of the war with his path to infamy then set fair. (*CD/Author*)

reported to his mother that, 'It would not have happened if I had been there.' To which his mother wrote, 'I can only agree with him. The two brothers generally flew side by side: they never lost sight of one another and each was the other's best protection.' In truth, there was nothing he could have done, but as we now appreciate survivor's guilt is a crippling condition.

Lothar returned to JG I on 19 July as commander of Jasta 11 and by 12 August had increased his score to forty. The next day he was hit in his right leg by long-range fire from an American pilot with the 148th Aero Squadron flying a Sopwith Camel. Despite being crippled by this latest wound and haemorrhaging blood badly, he brought his Fokker D.VII down to a safe landing. He was quickly transported to the nearest field hospital and, when triaged, taken to Hamburger Vereinsshospital for specialist treatment. He was then sent home to Schweidnitz to be nursed by his mother and sister. It was here that he received word that the war had ended.

Like many veterans, Lothar seems to have found adjusting to peace difficult. A marriage to Countess Doris von Keyserlingk in June 1919 did not last, although quickly produced two children – Carmen Viola on 12 May 1920 and Wolf Manfred in March 1922 – before the couple separated that year. It seems likely that his restless, unsettled state of mind after the war may have been the cause of disputes and caused a parting of

Lothar's return to front-line flying in July 1918 was very active but only too brief. (Above left) A photo apparently taken on the eve of his departure for JG I reveals changes to his face resulting from the serious facial wounds he sustained on 13 March. By this time Fokker D.VIIs were available in large numbers and here (above right) Lothar is seen with his father and a D.VII he flew on occasions. (Lower left) Preparing for flight in the same aircraft. On 13 August he was shot down and sustained a leg wound that ended his war. (Lower right) Lothar poses with Hermann Göring (right), who commanded JG I until the end of the war, and Bruno Loerzer, who led JG III during 1918. (*CD/Author*)

the ways. There would be no reconciliation because in the same year he was killed when ferrying the actress Fern Andra and her manager between Berlin and Hamburg. After unsuccessfully trying to become an estate manager, then working in industry, he returned to what he knew best and became a pilot. In this case he found employment with the fledgling Deutsche Luft-Reederei, which was developing a service carrying passengers and mail in old war surplus aircraft. And it was in an LVG C.VI that he met his death on 22 July and was buried beside his father close to the family home in Schweidnitz. One can only imagine the sense of loss Kunigunde must have felt at losing her husband and two of her children in such a short time. However, she was nothing but resilient and survived some very difficult years as best she could, with a small military pension, which was soon denuded by rampart inflation, and the royalties from Manfred's autobiography.

To supplement her income, and provide a lasting memorial to her two sons, Kunigunde created a small museum in her home that attracted visitors from home and abroad. And

Lothar found readjusting to civilian life in a country close to revolution difficult, as different parties sought to dominate Germany's future. For someone trained to be a soldier and a fighter pilot, a demilitarised nation could offer him little in the way of employment. (Above left) In June 1919 he married Doris von Keyserlingk – seen here with his parents and sister behind and to his right. It proved to be a short-lived union and although producing two children ended in separation during 1922. (Above right) In most pictures of Lothar he seems to have adopted a stony expression (including his wedding picture), perhaps being made uncomfortable by the revealing nature of photographs. Here, in May 1921, he seems more at ease with himself at a German Aviator Commemoration Day event in Munich, where he met many old comrades. (*CD/Author*)

When an opportunity arose to fly again, albeit as a civilian, he jumped at the chance, but sadly perished on 22 July 1922, when the engine of the LVG he was flying failed and it crashed, killing its pilot. (*CD*)

After the war Manfred's grave at Bertangles fell into a state of neglect and was treated very roughly by the local population, who had suffered for many years because of Germany's invasion in 1914. The beautifully carved cross and metal plaque of April 1918 soon disappeared, to be replaced by this rather crude version. As both sides gradually retrieved their dead from the battlefield and gathered them together, Manfred's body was transferred to Fricourt and Germany's communal cemetery there. (*Author*)

As a memorial to her sons, Kunigunde von Richthofen, with the help of her surviving children, created a museum in her home and filled it with the many souvenirs collected by Manfred and Lothar during the war. These rooms were also graced by the many works of art commissioned during the war for public display. During the Soviet advance into Germany in 1944–45 the house was ransacked and most of this collection disappeared; Kunigunde and her daughter having been forced to flee with very few possessions before the enemy arrived. (*CD*)

Berlin 20 November 1925 and Manfred's body is brought to the capital for a state funeral and then laid to rest in the national Invalidenfriedhof Cemetery among other German heroes. Such was the importance of the occasion that Paul von Hindenburg, now president, attended along with many of Manfred's comrades, acting as pall bearers. Here Kunigunde, with her surviving son and daughter, walk slowly behind the coffin, followed by von Hindenburg, as they approach the cemetery for Manfred's interment. The last photograph in this group shows the cross erected over Manfred's grave in the German communal cemetery at Fricourt in France immediately after the war when his body was moved there from Bertangles. It was retrieved by his brother, Bolko, and then placed on display in Berlin. (*CD/Author*)

in the inter-war years Manfred's status did not fade in Germany, Britain and the USA, in particular. This was helped by two biographies and numerous other items written about him that appeared, plus his repatriation from France to his homeland. His mother had hoped for a quite exhumation from a communal cemetery at Fricourt, where Manfred's body had been moved shortly after the war, and reburial beside his father and brother. But this was not to be. His remains were claimed by the state and a funeral full of pomp and ceremony in Berlin on 20 November 1925, ordered and arranged by the powers that be. He was then laid to rest in the Invalidenfriedhof Cemetery, over which was placed a simple commemorative stone.

So Manfred may have remained undisturbed in his grave as his deeds faded into history and legend. But the potency of the image created in the Great War was too strong to be ignored as Germany sleepwalked into a Nazi-fuelled dark age. With Hermann Göring leading a revitalised and rapidly expanding Luftwaffe, the memory of the country's greatest hero and symbol of its fighting spirit was soon enlisted by a new generation of propagandists. Yet even here his name could not be sullied by such an association and the respect with which he was held, at home and abroad, did not diminish and survived yet another world war intact. Sadly, though, his grave, now pockmarked with bullets, remained out of bounds when Berlin was divided into zones and the Berlin Wall was erected. Meanwhile, in Schweidnitz, all trace of Albrecht and Lothar's graves were swept away and rendered anonymous as Silesia was absorbed into a reborn Poland.

Neither Kunigunde nor her surviving children would see their country unified and be able to visit the graves of their loved ones. Kunigunde retired to live in Wiesbaden, where she died on the 24 April 1962, aged 93, soon to be followed by her daughter during January 1963 at her home at Cuxhaven. Ilse married Major Karl von Reibnitz after the war and gave birth to two daughters, Anna and Nicol, and a son, Manfred. Widowhood followed when Karl died aged 51 in 1929 and she did not remarry. In 1931, Bolko married Viktoria von Richthofen, a distant relative, became a successful businessman and often visited the USA, before and after the Second World War. He and Viktoria had two sons – Manfred and Hartmann – before they divorced. He lived in Karlsruhe until his death in December 1971 aged 68, and was then buried beside his mother, there to finally be joined by Manfred in 1975 when permission was gained to remove his body from the no man's land created by the Berlin Wall.

Apart from a few memorials there is little to remind us of this time of great endeavour when the skies above the Western Front were a dangerous place to be. It was a time when only the skilled and the lucky survived and many hundreds perished in the most terrible ways when fortune went against them.

Those who chose the skies over the slaughter and filth of the trenches did so in the certain knowledge that their chances of survival were far less than the millions fighting on the ground beneath them. And still they went up each day to seek battle no matter what the cost. Manfred von Richthofen, by luck and judgement, became a master of this perilous art and led a group of like-minded men with courage and resolve against an equally redoubtable enemy. In so doing he became a German hero and an icon whose reputation even leapt national boundaries to rise above a natural malice towards a foe, eventually sublimating into a deep admiration that has lasted to this day.

During the 1930s the Nazis were quick to enlist Manfred's image to their cause. (Above left and right) Here Hermann Göring makes a hugely ostentatious show of remembering the Great War hero and one of his predecessors as commander of JG I, seemingly ignoring Manfred's mother, sister and brother in the process. (Below) Even Kunigunde found herself having to play her part in Nazi propaganda, in this case 'christening' a new glider. Between the wars the 1919 Treaty of Versailles banned Germany from operating an air force. So to train pilots for the day when the new Luftwaffe could be unveiled young men took to the air in gliders, hence Kunigunde's participation as mother of the service's greatest hero in this scheme. (*Author*)

In the post-war years Kunigunde, with great resolve and stoicism, began a new life far away from her old home in Silesia. It seems that Fern Andra, with whom she is pictured here in the 1950s, became an occasional visitor. To the end of her life she was eager to recall her two gallant sons and remind later generations of their existence and their courage. (*CD*)

# Bibliography

Armstrong, Harry G, "The Principles & Practice of Aviation Medicine," Balliere (1952).

Barbusse, Henri, "Under Fire," Penguin Books (2003).

Bishop, W A, "Winged Warfare," Hodder & Stoughton (1918).

Bodenschatz, Karl, "Jagd in Flanderns Himmel," (1935).

Burrows, William E, "Richthofen," Hart-Davis (1969).

Carisella, P J, "Who Killed the Red Baron," White Lion (1974).

Clark, Christopher, "The Iron Kingdom," Penguin (2006).

Culpin, M, "Psychoneurosis of War and Peace," Cambridge (1920).

Davies, Belinda J, "Home Fires Burning," University of North Carolina (2000).

Fenton, N R, "Shell Shock and its Aftermath," St Louis (1926).

Ferko, A E, "Richthofen," (1995).

Fokker, Anthony, "Flying Dutchman," George Routledge (1934).

Franks, Norman, "Jasta Boelke," Grub Street (2004).

Franks, Norman, "Sky Tiger," William Kimber (1980).

Gibbons, Floyd, "The Red Knight of Germany," Cassall (1930).

Grinker, Roy, "Men Under Stress," Skilled Books (1945).

Hawker, Tyrrel, "Hawker VC," Pen and Sword (2013).

Henden. H & Haas. A P, "Wounds of War. The Psychological Aftermath of Combat in the Vietnam War," New York (1986).

Hegender, Heinz, "Fokker. The Man and His Aircraft," Harleyford (1961).

Hillier-Graves, Tim, "Heaven High, Ocean Deep," Casemate (2019).

Hillier-Graves, Tim, "Widowmaker," Casemate (2020).

Italiander, Rolf, "Richthofen," Verlag Berlin (1938).

Johnson, J E, "Wing Leader," Goodall Publications (1956).

Kilduff, Peter, "The Red Baron," David & Charles (2007).

Kilduff, Peter, "Richthofen. Beyond the Legend," Arms and Armour (1993).

Kilduff, Peter, "The Red Baron's Combat Wing," Arms and Armour (1997).

Lasswell, Harold, "Propaganda in the World War," Martono Publishing (1938).

Lee, Arthur Gould, "No Parachute," Jarrolds (1968).

Lee, Arthur Gould, "Open Cockpit," Jarrolds (1969).

Lee, John, "The War Lords," (Weidenfield & Nicolson (2005).

Ludendorff, Erich, "The Concise Ludendorff Memoirs," Hutchison (1935).

Marson, T B, "Scarlet and Khaki," Jonathan Cape (1930).

McKee, Alexander, "The Friendless Sky," Souvenir Press (1962).

Nowarra, Heinz & Brown, Kimborough S, "Von Richthofen & The Flying Circus," Harleyford (1965).

Robinson, Douglas H, "The Dangerous Sky," Foulis (1973).

Rochford, Leonard H, "I Chose the Sky," William Kimber (1977).

Schroder, Hans, "An Airman Remembers," Aviation Book Club (1933).

Sheppard, Ben, "The War of Nerves," Jonathan Cape (2000).

Stokes, Doug, "Paddy Finucane. Fighter Ace," William Kimber (1983).

Taylor, A J P, "The First World War," Hamish Hamilton (1963).

Taylor, P M, "Munitions of the Mind," Manchester University Press (1990).

Titler, Dale M, "The Day the Red Baron Died,"Ian Allan (1970).

Udet, Ernst, "Mein Fliegerleben," Ullstein (1935)

Vigilant, "Richthofen. The Red Knight of Germany," John Hamilton (1935).

Von Richthofen, Kunigunde, "Mein Kriegstagebuch," (1937).

Von Richthofen, Manfred, "Derr Rote Kampflieger," Ullstien (1917).

Wenzl, Richard, "Richthofen Flieger", Badische Zeitung (1918/1930).

Werner, Johannes, "Knight of Germany," Greenhill Books (1991).

Weyl, A R, "Fokker. The Creative Years," Putnams (1965).

Williamson, Henry, "A Fox Under My Cloak," MacDonald (1956).

Winter, Denis, "First of the Few," Allen Lane (1982).

Wyngarden, Greg van, "The Richthofen Circus," Osprey (2004).

# Index

Dear Reader,

We hope you have enjoyed this book, but why not share your views on social media? You can also follow our pages to see more about our other products: facebook.com/penandswordbooks or follow us on X @penswordbooks

You can also view our products at www.pen-and-sword.co.uk (UK and ROW) or www.penandswordbooks.com (North America).

To keep up to date with our latest releases and online catalogues, please sign up to our newsletter at: www.pen-and-sword.co.uk/newsletter

If you would like a printed catalogue with our latest books, then please email: enquiries@pen-and-sword.co.uk or telephone: 01226 734555 (UK and ROW) or email: uspen-and-sword@casematepublishers.com or telephone: (610) 853-9131 (North America).

We respect your privacy and we will only use personal information to send you information about our products.

Thank you!